HE
WILL NEVER
GIVE UP ON
YOU!
NEVER?
NEVER!

HE
WILL NEVER
GIVE UP ON
YOU!
NEVER?
NEVER!

JOE BARNETT

COVENANT
PUBLISHING

Unless otherwise indicated, Scripture quotations used in this book are from The Holy Bible, New International Version, copyright © 1978 by New York International Bible Society.

Other Scripture references are from the following sources:

J.B. Phillips (JBP): The New Testament in Modern English, copyright © 1958, Macmillan Publishing Co., Inc.

The Message (MSG), copyright © 1993, NavPress Publishing Group.

New American Standard Bible (NASB), copyright © 1960, 1977 by the Lockman Foundation.

The Holy Bible, New Century Version (NCV), copyright © 1987, 1988, 1991 by Word Publishing, Nashville, Tennessee.

The Holy Bible, New Living Translation (NLT), copyright © 1996, Tyndale House Publishers, Inc., Wheaton, Illinois.

The New Revised Standard Version of the Bible (NRSV), copyright © 1989 by the Division of Christian Education of the National Council of the Churches of Christ in the USA.

The Good News Bible: The Bible in Today's English Version (TEV), copyright © 1976 by the American Bible Society.

The Living Bible (TLB), copyright © 1971 by Tyndale House Publishers, Wheaton, Illinois.

DEDICATION

To Mother and Daddy

You introduced me to Jesus,
knowing that little else matters.

I am eternally (literally) grateful.

TABLE OF CONTENTS

ACKNOWLEDGEMENTS

I am a part of all that I have met," wrote Tennyson.

So am I . But more fortunate than most, for those I have met are the best. They have strengthened me, inspired me, shaped me.

This book has my name on the cover, but in truth it is the work of many—of those who have nudged me to put thoughts into words onto paper. To a few of these, I offer a word of thanks.

To Jack cardwell. For your belief in me two decades ago. without your encouraging , supportive friendship none of my words would ever have seen print.

To Allen Isbell. For being my unfailing friend for nearly half a century. Not once in all these years have I heard a discouraging word from you. Remarkable! (In the chapter *"Let's Be Friends"* there is a section that was inspired by your treasured friendship.)

To Cindy Verdone. For first-proofing. Especially for helping me with what I've never figured out—where to put the commas.

To Gene Shelburne. For your sharp mind, sharp eyes, and sharp blue pencil. You have long been one of my favorite writers, and there is no one I'd rather have edit my work.

To Edwin White and Steve Cable of Covenant Publishing.

For your confidence. I admire your hard work, your courage, your vision, your passion, and your integrity.

To Fred and Jan Alexander, Mary Jo Bauman, Horace and Dott Coffman, Phil and Beth Crumpler, Ted Dockery, Dan and Jo Ann Flemming, Bob and Eloise Fowler, Douglas "Fessor" Fry, Jerry and Judy Gallagher, Rosemary Garza, John and Beth Gipson, Hazel Newton, Fred Rorex, Mary Ann Thompson, Ron Willingham, Jay and Dianna Wischkaemper. Each of you knows What you've done. On second thought, you probably don't, since encouragement is second nature to your unassuming spirit. What would I do without you? One of the great blessings of my life is that I don't have to—do without you, I mean.

To each of you, my heartfelt gratitude.

FOREWORD

Jason just left my office. He wanted something—but he couldn't tell me what, because he doesn't know. He only knows that in his heart there is an aching hunger, a gnawing need.

Jason's hungry heart will stir a sympathetic vibration in some of my readers who are feeling the same emptiness. Feeling that something is missing, that life is lacking.

It is my prayer that as you thumb through these pages you will find a morsel here and there that will help relieve your hunger.

In the quiet hours of writing this book, I have envisioned it not in the hands of hundreds, but in the hands of only one. And they are yours.

You may not remember it, but one of those little blue and white cards with Morgan Nick's picture on it, asking *Have You Seen Me?* probably showed up in your mail box.

It has been over two years since Morgan, the 6-year-old daughter of Colleen Nick, disappeared from an Arkansas ballpark. As I write these words, Morgan hasn't been found. But

Colleen vows she will never give up. "I would never want to look her in the eye and tell her I didn't believe enough," she says. The porch light stays on every night at Colleen's house.

The assertion of this book is that Jesus will never look you in the eye and tell you that he gave up. He will keep the porch light on until you are safely home.

He will never give up on you!

Never?

Never!

PROLOGUE

hen the fullness of the time came, God sent forth His Son, born of a woman (Galatians 4:4 NASB). And the Word became flesh, and dwelt among us. . . (John 1:14 NASB).

"Son, it's time."

"The fullness of time?"

"Yes, the fullness of time."

The son's mind drifted back to that million-years-ago conversation that they had had about the fullness of time. It had seemed strange to talk about time, for then there was no time. No years, months, weeks. No clock. No calendar.

It was when earth was nothing but a formless mass, blanketed in darkness.

Before the waters were gathered into seas and dry land appeared.

Before grass, trees, flowers.

Before sun, moon, stars.

Before fish, birds, animals.

Before Adam.

Before . . . time.

He remembered how they had transformed the dark empty Earth into a dazzling world of wonder.

"Let there be light!" God had ordered. And there was light.

They had divided light from darkness, and days were born. Days that stretched into weeks, and months, and years. And there was . . . time.

They had created plants. And animals. (He smiled as he recalled shaping the hippopotamus, the hedgehog, and the hyena—and then saddling Adam with the task of naming them.)

Then God had said, *"Let us make a man."* And he remembered how a shadow had crossed the father's face. He was looking into the future, and he didn't like what he saw—the man rebelling. Sinning. Dying.

Dying? Man wasn't made to die. He was made to live—forever. *"Let us make someone like ourselves,"* God had said. Timeless. Eternal.

But the devil would lie, and the man would die.

And the shadow had crossed the father's face because he knew the remedy would be radical—the sacrifice of heaven's best.

The eyes of father and son had met. Heaven's first tears fell. The father wept. The angels anguished. The son sighed.

"I'll go," he had said.

"It's a horrible step to take—from deity to dirt," said the father.

"I'll go."

"It will be brutal."

"I'll go."

"You will have to endure hatred, rejection, betrayal, torture . . . and . . ."

"And death. The cross. I know. I'll go. When do I leave?"

"In the fullness of time."

The design was flawless. Every piece in place—from the cradle, to the cross, to the crypt.

To man, the project would be incomprehensible. Mysterious. Bizarre. But it was heaven's way. The only way.

He smiled again as he thought about their plan for his earth entry. He would make his debut as a baby . . . born to a virgin mother. (The only baby ever to choose his own mother and his own name.)

His arrival would be unannounced, except to a handful of stargazers and shepherds. An extraterrestrial trio—an angel, a heavenly choir, and a star—would reveal his birth to them.

The star!

He recalled what the father had said about the star—it had to appear at exactly the right place at exactly the right time.

"Earth will be there," he had said, pointing into nothingness. *"And the star will be there,"* he had said, pointing to another spot in the blackness.

It will take . . . let's see . . . it will take the light of the star 931,000 years, 12 days, 3 hours, 21 minutes, and 47 seconds to get to exactly the right spot. We must birth her now!" He snapped his fingers, and the star blazed into being.

The light from the star was on its way, before there was an Earth, an Adam, a Nazareth, a Bethlehem. The light that would guide the magi to the manger would have been speeding its way toward earth for nearly a million years when they first saw it.

His reflection was interrupted by the father's voice.

"Son, it's time."

"Is the virgin ready?"

"Gabriel is in Nazareth now, telling her the plan."

"And?"

"Confused. Disturbed. But, as always, submissive to our will. We chose well when we chose her."

15

"And the angels?"

"Ready to announce. Ready to sing."

"I will miss you, Father."

"And I, you. More than I can tell you."

They embraced. And the son moved out of heaven, and into the virgin's womb. From Emperor to embryo.

CHAPTER 1

WHAT A NIGHT!

He stood on the porch of the Inn, legs apart in an at-ease position, glad his watch was ending. A pale wash of light was just beginning to break in the lower eastern sky. A rooster crowed. A bird fluttered.

"The air feels good, eh?" he said to the soldier who had come to replace him.

"Colder'n a Pharisee!" he growled, pulling his scarf tight and stuffing the ends into his jacket.

They resented being assigned to Bethlehem, the ragged edge of nowhere. This would be just another day, passed in boredom and then casually put away.

"Anything hap'nin'?" he asked, cackling with undisguised scorn.

"Nah. Oh, there's been some chatter about a transient birthin' a baby in the barn behind the Inn last night," he said, jerking his thumb toward the stable. "Nothin' important ever happens around here."

Christmas season is in full swing. Nativity scenes are being lugged from basements and attics and assembled in front yards and church yards. Reminders of the Bethlehem-happening.

In the mall this morning I was drawn to a group of caroling children. Cherubic faces scrubbed, they had come to sing. And did they ever sing! What was lacking in melody was made up in volume. *O little town of Bethlehem,* they screeched, *How still we see thee lie!*

These pint-size performers from a little West Texas town know next to nothing about New York, Paris, or London. But Bethlehem? They know about Bethlehem.

That "nothin' important" Bethlehem night turned history on its ear. But if you and I had been there that night we, like that soldier, wouldn't have sensed anything unusual. Tonight would have seemed no different from last night. Or from the same night last week. Or last year. Nothing marked this night as remarkable. No banners. No bands. No fireworks.

Just the same old routine.

Frazzled moms slumped and sighed, *Thank God!* as their boisterous broods drifted into dreamland.

Drained dads labored over ledgers, trying to make ends meet.

Camels and cattle blew puffs of mist as they were watered, foddered, and bedded down for the night.

Shepherds tucked their cloaks under their chins, shielding against the biting winter wind. They watched their flocks out of the corners of alert and experienced eyes, and washed down stale bread with cold coffee.

I know it seems far-fetched, but it was here in this isolated field of sheep and shepherds that the birth of Jesus was first announced. These shabby sheepherders were the first to hear about the arrival of the Messiah.

Some wag chirped that if God had asked her advice, she would have suggested a little more pizzaz in the announcement.

Maybe so. How would you feel if you were the lead soprano in the choir that announced his birth? You have been rehearsing for a couple of hundred years for this performance—two-a-days, sometimes three. You've been waiting in the wings for a century. Costumed. Coiffured. Confident!

Finally . . .

"He's born!" Gabriel shouts. *"You're on!"*

Up goes the curtain, and you see the crowd.

The crowd?! You've got to be kidding! The crowd—the whole crowd—is a handful of smelly shepherds. Hey! Who was in charge of publicity??!!

But the show must go on. And what a show it was![1]

Lights: The glory of the Lord shone around them.

Angel: I bring you the most joyful news ever announced . . . The Savior—yes, the Messiah, the Lord—has been born tonight in Bethlehem!

Chorus: Glory to God in the highest heaven, and peace on earth . . .

Finale: Angels make a breath-taking exit into heaven.

Successful show? You be the judge. Look at the effect it had on the crowd. Those shepherds did what shepherds never do. Never! They forsook their flocks. "Let's go to Bethlehem and see this thing that has happened," they said.

So they hurried off and found Mary and Joseph, and the baby, who was lying in the manger.

God Is With Us

What a night!

It is so simple that you can get the whole story on a 4 x 6-inch Christmas card. And so complex that across the hall I have 257 linear feet of shelves, filled with books by generations of scholars who have scarcely scratched the surface of the story.

This was the night that the world had been waiting for since God vowed that the seed of woman would crush Satan (Genesis 3:15)

And since he promised Abraham that in his lineage would be one who would bless all nations (Galatians 3:16),

And since Moses pledged that a greater prophet than he would one day come (Deuteronomy 18:15-18),

And since Isaiah prophesied that *"a child shall be born to a virgin! And she shall call him Immanuel (meaning, 'God is with us')"* (Isaiah 7:14).

God is with us! Read that line slowly. *God . . . is . . . with . . . us!*

Look at that baby in the manger. He looks like any other baby. But that baby is God—with blood and bones, eyes and ears, hands and hair.

What a night! The night that God swapped a castle for a cradle, divinity for humanity, heaven for hell.

Naming the Baby

"Congratulations Mr. Arnold, you have a son!"

"Okay."

"What is his name? I need it for the record."

"Doesn't matter to me. Just pick one."

"Seriously, Mr. Arnold, I need to record it. What is his name?"

"And seriously, Miss Nurse, I don't care. You name him."

"Okay. How about Judas?"

"Fine with me. Judas it is."

I don't think so! Naming the baby is serious business. Parents-to-be give sober thought to the name of their baby-to-be. The baby's name isn't a trivial tag. It establishes an identity, a standard. It commits the child to something.

You have heard, haven't you, of the Grecian coward whose name was Alexander? His commander, *Alexander the Great*, ordered him either to change his name or his conduct.

Did he do either? I don't know. But I'll tell you what I do know—Alexander the Coward didn't choose his name. His parents did. Alexander wasn't consulted.

But the Bethlehem baby chose his own name. Mary and Joseph weren't *asked* what their baby's name would be. They were *told*.

> . . .you shall name him Jesus (meaning 'Savior'), for he will save his people from their sins (Matthew 1:20-21 tlb).

The name he chose declared his mind and his mission: why he came, what he proposed to be and do. It identified his goal, committed him to something incredibly big—*He will save his people from their sins!*

Not, he *wants* to. Not, he *hopes* to. Not, he will *try* to. But, he *will!*

Not, he will keep his people from sinning. Not, he will reward his people for their righteousness. But, *he will save his people from their sins.*

That baby was not born because of your strength, but because of your sin. Not because of your goodness, but because of your guilt. Not because you take a stand, but because you took a fall.

There is no other Savior. Not goodness. Not works. Not rules, regulations, or rituals. These are substitute saviors. Don't trust your soul to them. Your only hope is Jesus, the one-and-only heaven-sent Savior.

You shall name him Jesus. When you invoke the name of Jesus, you appeal to him by his own word, by the name he himself chose: *Jesus—Savior.*

If you're not already sitting, you may want to take a chair, because I'm going to tell you a knee-buckling, heart-pounding truth . . .

He named himself with you in mind!

Really. Listen to the angel:

> I bring you the most joyful news ever announced, and it is for everyone! The Savior—yes, the Messiah, the Lord—has been born . . . (Luke 2:10-11, emphasis mine).

Did you get that? *It is for* **everyone**! You can write your name there.

I did. In my Bible it says: I *bring you the most joyful news ever announced, and it is for Joe Barnett!* (I penciled it in.)

In your Bible *your* name belongs there. So go ahead, write your name in the margin at Luke 2:10.

Prince of Peace

There is no peace where there is fear.

Luba Gercak can tell you that. Luba lived for years in fear. Fear that freedom would never come. Fear that peace would never be.

Luba grew up in a Jewish community in Poland. When war broke out, she and her husband and child were sucked into its deadly undertow. They were loaded into horse-drawn wagons for a nightmare trek to Auschwitz-Birkenau, the most hideous of the German concentration camps.

When they arrived at the camp, an SS guard wrenched

Luba's three-year-old from her arms and threw him on a truck packed with prisoners too young or too old to work. Luba wept bitterly as the truck rolled away to the gas chamber. And soon wept again as her husband also was executed.

Luba was sent to the Bergen-Belsen concentration camp, where one night she heard a child crying. Opening the barracks door she was stunned by the sight of a pack of terrified, shivering children—54 of them. Children whose fathers, mothers, and older siblings had been carted away to the camps of Auschwitz, Treblinka, or Chelmno. Then these children had been hauled to the Bergen-Belsen compound and kicked off the trucks.

Luba, risking her life, brought the tattered tots into the barracks. Each day she begged, bartered, and stole food for them. She nursed them when they were sick and sang lullabies to them when they cried.

Dysentery left the children dehydrated, limp with exhaustion, and vulnerable to the raging fever of typhus. Luba prayed for a miracle to save them.

It came after many months, on Sunday, April 15, 1945. A British tank column rolled into Bergen-Belsen with loudspeakers blaring: "You are free! You are free!"[2]

Peace at last!

One of the defining titles of Jesus is *Prince of Peace*.
For to us a child is born . . . And he will be called . . . Prince of Peace (Isaiah 9:6).

I repeat, there is no peace where there is fear. But you don't need Luba Gercak—or me—to tell you that. Some of you have lived in that prison for years. Afraid that you won't do enough. Afraid that you've done too much. Afraid of God. Afraid of judgment.

You cast a trembling glance at past sins and say, "*No chance!*"—a nervous peek at present flaws and say, "*No way!*"

And Jesus says, "*No problem!*"

Listen to the cry from the cradle: "You are free! You are free!"

"*Don't be afraid! . . . I bring you the most joyful news ever announced . . . The Savior . . . has been born tonight . . .*"

What a night!

CHAPTER 2

THE SEARCH IS ON

T he day was dismal, but the old man was cheerful—as
people with purpose usually are. Sloshing through ankle-
deep mud in the carnival camp, he peddled pictures and
proverbs to weary workers. With a tip of his hat and a respectful bow, he gave Rosalie Joyce's mother a picture of the Good
Shepherd, cradling the lost sheep in his arms.

Little Rosalie was captivated by that picture. Over and over
she explored it, tracing each line with her finger, while pondering the text beneath it:

. . . the Son of Man came to seek and to save what was lost.

Know what I wish? I wish I could sit down beside little Rosalie
and read to her, talk to her. I wish I could read her the chapter you
just finished. I would tell her how Satan, crafty devil that he is,
snookered Adam and Eve in Eden. I would explain how they fell
for his line, and began a business that would last until the end of
time—the funeral business.

But I would also tell her how God made a promise that day
that the devil wouldn't win, that one day a Savior—the Good
Shepherd in her picture—would come (see Genesis 3:14-15).
And sure enough, he did.

I would have to tell her, of course, that most folks missed him—
that only a few were aware that he was the promised Savior.

Mary knew because an angel told her (Luke 1:26-35).

Joseph knew because the angel told him, too (Matthew 1:21).

Elizabeth, Mary's six-months-pregnant cousin, knew because her baby leaped inside her when Mary came to visit (Luke 1:39-45).

Other than that, only a gaggle of shepherds and sages were aware (Matthew 2:1-2, Luke 2:8-11).

Nevertheless, he was here. On a finely-focused mission. As God had promised. As the picture in little Rosalie's hands proclaimed.

He Came To Seek the Lost

On a cold, blustery December afternoon Carla Cortez was doing laundry at Wan's Wash & Dry, a laundromat tucked into a small L-shaped shopping center in San Jose, California. Her son Edwin, a lively three-year-old, was playing in the waiting area.

When she finished folding a load of laundry, Carla walked across the room. "Where's Edwin?" she asked a friend who had come to the laundromat with them.

"He was just here," she replied, glancing around.

Carla quickly searched the room. No Edwin.

Heart pounding, she ran outside. No Edwin.

Racing through the shopping center, she yanked open the door of each store, screaming his name. No answer. No Edwin.

Where is my boy? Frantic, and bursting into tears, she dialed 911 at a pay phone. In minutes, six police units converged on the Laundromat. Fifteen officers, led by Sgt. Art Flores, began searching for Edwin.

Two hours later, still no Edwin.

Sgt. Flores was worried. Experience told him this was shaping up like an abduction. If a child snatched by a stranger was not found within a few hours, the search usually ended at a shallow grave.

They appealed for help on the evening news. By 9 p.m., in spite of drenching rain, more than 100 volunteers had arrived. With fistfuls of fliers bearing Edwin's picture, they hit the streets, handing them out and taping them to shop windows.

By midnight hope was fading.

Rosalia Varela, a waitress at Jalisco Taquería, glanced at the flier on the counter. *How sad*, she thought, gazing at Edwin's big dark eyes.

At 12:40 a.m., 20 minutes before closing time, Rosalia stepped outside. She noticed a small silver Toyota parked in the shadows. In the driver's seat was a man with frizzy brown hair. Next to him was a small Hispanic boy, his big dark eyes open wide. *The missing child!*

Within five minutes of Rosalia's call to the police, kidnapper Sergio Madriz Soto was in handcuffs, and Edwin was in his mother's arms.[1]

Relieved? Me too.

Your heart hurt for Carla Cortez as you read that story, didn't it? You felt her torment. Her anguish.

Torment! Anguish! That's what God feels when one of his children is missing. He will turn the world upside down to find his lost child. That's why he came. He didn't set up *Search Central* in heaven. He didn't issue orders from Paradise. He left luxury to personally lead the search . . . on Earth.

His strategy? He arranged his agenda and scheduled his steps to intersect the paths of the lost.

> He showed up at a well at high noon because that's where she would be—a disillusioned, five-times-married woman who was trying yet again (minus the marriage license) with number six (John 4:4-29).

He showed up under a sycamore tree because that's where he would be—a rich businessman who had it all, and was hoping to God that wasn't all there was (Luke 19:1-10).

He showed up at the Temple because that's where she would be—a trapped, terrified adulteress (John 8:1-11).

He showed up on a dusty road because that's where he would be—an arrogant churchman doing ungodly things in the name of God (Acts 9:1-20).

He showed up in a carnival camp because that's where she would be—a precious little girl named Rosalie.

Do you see? He finds the lost by putting himself in their path.

He came searching for you just as he did for them. And somehow, some way, he will put himself in front of you. Through sermon or solitude. Through success or failure. Joy or pain. Calm or storm. Some way.

You may at this very moment be holding in your hands the plan he designed to intersect your path. He may be smiling because he has brought you and this book together. Smiling because he has, at last, found you.

If not, his search will continue.

"The search has been called off!" It's hard to imagine more chilling words than those. That announcement is always made sadly, reluctantly. But when every lead has been exhausted and further effort seems futile, limited resources of funds, equipment, and personnel must be deployed to more promising possibilities.

But Jesus—this is a promise—Jesus will never call off the search for you. He will never give up. He came seeking you, and he won't quit until he finds you.

And even then he won't be finished. He has more in mind.

He Came to Save

Three-year-old Edwin Cortez could have been found in a shallow grave. Sought and found, but not saved.

Jesus won't settle for that. He didn't come to seek to save, but to seek *and* to save. He will settle for nothing less. If you think he is going to give up, think again. He will never give up on you!

Never?

Never!

I started tell you about Rosalie and the carnival a moment ago. Let me do that before I get sidetracked again.

I've read what the scholars have written, but little Rosalie's exposition of the text is as good as I've seen.[2]

Chatting with Jinx, a friend from another caravan, she said, "You see, Jinx, there are only two kinds of sheep. The ones that are safe, and the ones that are lost."

"Is that all the kinds?"

"Yes. Why?"

"Well," replied Jinx, "I've done lots of bad things. I've got into tempers, and I've sworn. So I must be a lost sheep. That's a dreadful thing to be, isn't it?"

"Yes, dreadful," said Rosalie sadly. "But if you're a lost sheep," she then said excitedly, "if you're a lost sheep, you are the very one that Jesus came to save, because he came to seek and to save what was lost!"

Last Sunday a preacher somewhere preached on that text. I don't know what he said, but I'm sure he said nothing better than that.

CHAPTER 3

HE BELIEVES IN YOU

*S*he believed in me!"

That's what Henry Ward Beecher said about a teacher who taught only one year in the rural elementary school he attended. Her belief in him put his feet on the path to greatness. He said she was responsible for whatever success he had achieved.

It's a common ingredient in the lives of people who succeed. Someone believed in them. A parent. Grandparent. Teacher. Friend. Someone.

Encouragement may be a one-time gift, but it often pays lifetime dividends.

It did for Stanley Mooneyham.

Stanley was born a few years before the Depression, the seventh child of a tenant farmer who could barely write his name. He wore hand-me-down clothes, took biscuits and fried sweet potatoes to school for lunch, and stood in food lines with his mother for government handouts to poor families.

This painful partnership with poverty produced a miserably low self-image in Stanley, resulting in a speech stammer so severe that he couldn't answer any questions orally in class. He had to write his answers on the chalkboard.

During this black period of his life, Mrs. Beasley, the County

37

Superintendent of Schools, showed special interest in Stanley. Periodically she would tell his teacher to have him come by her office after school. He lived for those visits. Mrs. Beasley believed in him.

Since his stammer made oral communication torturous, Stanley decided to become a writer. One day he shoved a few pages of his work in front of Mrs. Beasley. She read. And gushed! "Stanley, you are going to be a writer," she said. "This is good!" And she meant it. "Now you keep on writing, you hear? I want to put your books on my shelf."

Mrs. Beasley didn't live long enough to put Stanley's books on her shelf. But the thing that kept him writing through enough rejection slips to paper your living room wall was that Mrs. Beasley believed he was a writer. The publishers might not think so, but Mrs. Beasley did. She believed in him!

Dr. Stanley Mooneyham's name is on the covers of dozens of books. "Every one of them," he says, "is a tribute to a woman who believed in a little kid who was too shy and too scared to believe in himself."

Womack.
Mitchell.
Nelson.

Those names probably don't mean anything to you. But they mean a lot to me. Let me explain.

Mrs. Womack was my first-grade Sunday School teacher in San Angelo, Texas. I don't remember much about her. I don't remember her looks, her voice, her carriage, how she dressed, or how she fixed her hair. Do you know what I *do* remember? I remember that she made me feel important. Special. She believed in me!

Vance Mitchell was my Sunday School teacher when I was in junior high school in Midland, Texas. He was big, and *didn't take no guff from nobody!* Those were the only requirements for the job. (The leaders who recruited him weren't looking for someone who could *teach*—just for someone who could *control.*)

He could have easily bullied us into submission. But he didn't. He didn't need to. Know why? He believed in us!

We changed so dramatically under his coaching that the leaders in that little church did something I'm sure they never thought they would do. They asked Vance Mitchell's boys to make ten-minute talks to the church on Wednesday nights. It had all the marks of a miracle! (Except we didn't believe in miracles.)

When Vance Mitchell asked me to make one of those talks, I was scared silly. But he believed in me, and I couldn't let him down. I spent hours, days, working on my talk. Practiced for weeks to get it to exactly ten minutes. And got it down to the second. No sweat!

I said it in front of the mirror. Ten minutes!

I said it to the fence. Ten minutes!

I said it to my pet duck (really). Ten minutes!

And I said it to the church on Wednesday night. *Four minutes!*

I was horrified. I wanted to die, but was too busy throwing up in the parking lot. I never wanted to face anyone in that church again. I was trying to put distance between me and the church house when Clarence Nelson caught up with me. That gentle, kind man put his finger under my chin and lifted my head until he was looking me in the eye. "Joe," he said, "that was an outstanding talk! Just outstanding. I hope you'll be a preacher. You have what it takes to make a good one." He believed in me!

Mrs. Womack. Vance Mitchell. Clarence Nelson. God bless them! They believed in me.

But Jesus—ah—Jesus was the ultimate encourager. He believed in everyone—saw star quality even in poor performance.

Just ahead, the testimonies of a quartet of losers. An adulteress. A businessman. A divorcee. And a preacher. They have leading roles in later chapters of this book, but they are making cameo appearances in this chapter because—well, because Jesus believed in them. And it changed them forever.

The Adulteress:

I really thought it was all over—that they were going to kill me. They threw me in the dirt at the feet of Jesus. *"We caught her in bed with another woman's husband,"* they shrilled. *"Moses said stone her to death. What do you say?"*

Frankly, at that point I couldn't have cared less what he said. Or, for that matter, what they did to me. Would anyone care if they killed me? Would anyone—*anyone*—miss me? Would the world be better off without me? So many men. So many mistakes. So much pain. So much guilt. Another day, another blunder. So what?

Suddenly Jesus was standing. Staring. Speaking.

He who never sinned may throw the first stone at her.

I couldn't believe my ears. Had he really said what I thought he said? Must have, 'cause they dropped the rocks and hit the road. Every last one of them.

He was looking at me. Smiling.

"Where are they? Has no one condemned you?"

"No, sir," I said.

"Neither do I. Go and sin no more."

That was it? That was all?

I came limping and left skipping. This merciful man, whoever he was (and I really didn't know at the time), believed in me!

The Businessman:

I was perched on a tree limb when I saw him coming. For a long time I had wanted to see him, though I couldn't have told you why. These messiahs came and went, and held little interest for me.

But something was missing in my life. I had a hole in my soul. My self-image was the pits. And I was lonely. I had no friends. Not one. Money can't buy friends. Lord knows, I had plenty of money. Full pockets and an empty life.

He looked at me like he knew me. Surely not. How could he have known me? Clairvoyance? Nah! If that was it, he would have known to steer clear of me. I was pond scum in that town.

Then he spoke.

Zacchaeus! Come down! For I am going to be a guest in your home today!

My heart was hammering double-time. I don't know exactly how to say this, but I felt a stirring of self-worth that I hadn't felt in years, if ever. I didn't understand it then—and don't fully understand it now—but for some reason he believed in me.

The Divorcee:

I usually went to the well early in the morning, when it was cool. That's when everyone went. But I had decided that day to wait until the gossips were gone. I was weary of the whispers.

Forgive my vanity, but I used to be quite pretty. Not

anymore. At this point my looks were fast fading from fast living. My eyes had lost their sparkle and were framed by dark circles. My coal-black hair was showing streaks of gray. Every morning, it seemed, a new wrinkle appeared. Hard-earned wages of a wasted life.

I had worn five different names in the past seventeen years. For the life of me I couldn't make a marriage work. So now I was shacking up with number six. Why bother going through a ceremony? With my record it wouldn't last anyway. Besides, I couldn't think of anyone who would come to the wedding.

The clock chimed twelve times. Noon. It was hellishly hot. There wouldn't be anyone there now, so I trudged to the well.

That's where I met him. I was shocked when he spoke to me. You see, I'm a Samaritan—which means that with a Jew I clock in somewhere south of pork.

And "shocked" isn't strong enough to describe my reaction to what happened next. Understand I had never seen this man. *Never!* And he talked to me like he had known me all my life. He knew everything about me. *Everything!* Knew about my five husbands—and about the guy I was living with. And it didn't seem to matter. I mean, he didn't mark me off because of it.

He was the kindest man I ever met. He told me about eternal life—and offered it to me. To me, a five-time loser. Can you believe it? In a 10-minute conversation he turned my life around. I was—and still am—ecstatic. He . . . he believed in me.

The Preacher:

It's still hard for me to talk about. If anyone should have been strong enough to stand up and cry *foul* when they took him to trial, it was me. But I didn't. In fact, I denied even knowing him. Not once, but three times. Three times! And this while he was getting ready to die for me.

He told me it was going to happen, but I didn't believe him. I was too strong for that. "Not a chance!" I crowed. "I'll never deny you. These other guys might. Probably will. But they're not made of the same stuff as me. I'll die with you before I'll deny you!"

What I did broke my heart. You know, the thing that hurt the worst was knowing that I had hurt him, that I had violated his unfailing friendship.

I didn't know what I was going to do. Go back to fishing I supposed. I was quite sure that I was out! That he would never trust me again. But I was wrong about that. The most exhilarating words I ever heard were relayed to me by the women who went to the tomb on that first Easter morning:

> . . . go and give this message to his disciples including Peter: "Jesus is going ahead of you to Galilee. You will see him there . . ."

Including Peter! Did you hear that?! I was beside myself! Including Peter! Just two words, but I knew what he was saying: "You made a mistake my friend. It's okay. Everyone does. It is forgiven. I have an important assignment, and you're the man for the job. I need to talk to you about it. Let's do lunch."

I promised so valiantly, fell so wretchedly, and was received back so mercifully. He still believed in me!

Well, there they are!

A woman who answered her loneliness with her body instead of her brains.

A well-heeled businessman who spent his days with greed and his nights with guilt.

A woman with five hyphens in her last name.

And a cocksure clergyman who took a tumble.

All had one thing in common: they blew it!

Make that two things: they blew it—and Jesus believed in them!

Do you hear what they are saying to you? What he is saying to you?

You may have given up on yourself. I hope not. Because Jesus won't. He believes in you.

He will never give up on you!

Never?

Never!

CHAPTER 4

AN ARM AROUND YOUR SHOULDER

E very stadium became an echo chamber of catcalls when he jogged onto the field. Derision was deafening when he stepped into the batter's box. He was black—the first black to play major league baseball. Jackie Robinson.

He preferred to play at home in Brooklyn, where there were no boos, jeers, or racial slurs. *Until he made a mistake!* And he did, of course. Misjudged a sizzling grounder. A trickle of taunts swelled into a cacophony of contempt. The stands turned savage. Fists flashed. Curses flew. Bottles and half-eaten hot dogs sailed onto the field.

Jackie stood at second base, head down, humiliated.

Shortstop "Pee Wee" Reese took off his cap and slowly walked to Robinson's side. Putting his arm around his shoulder, he pierced the crowd with a steady stare. The stands became as quiet as a graveyard.

That arm around his shoulder, Jackie would later say, saved his career.

You've felt that need haven't you? The need for an arm around your shoulder? For someone to face your humiliation with you? Or your sorrow? Your loneliness?

Zacchaeus did.[1]

Zacchaeus was the most detested person in town. Scum.

Lowlife. Cheat. *Tax collector*—the person people loved to hate.

Early this morning he was sitting on the deck of his mansion, thumbing through his ledger. A good month, on target for a record year.

His thoughts were disrupted by unnerving crowd noise. He was accustomed to a smattering of picketing protesters. It came with the territory. But this was different. What had started as a murmur had swelled into a roar. "What's happening?" he wondered aloud.

"The Nazarene is in town," his secretary explained.

The Nazarene—Jesus. Zacchaeus had wondered about him for months. Nearly three years actually. Ever since Matthew, one of his tax-collecting cohorts, had walked away from his plush position and joined up with the man. From pariah to parson, crook to Christian.

Zacchaeus wanted to get a look at Jesus. So he slipped into the street, hoping to melt into the crowd and go unnoticed. Fat chance. He was about as inconspicuous as a celebrity in a soup line. He smelled of Old Spice and wore enough jewelry to stock a store.

A widow recognized him and bitterly hissed his name. Zacchaeus had squeezed her husband into bankruptcy—and her husband had escaped his humiliation by hanging himself on a frayed rope in an isolated fig tree. When she spoke Zacchaeus' name, heads turned. Hands hardened into fists. Lips curled in contempt. Curses turned the air blue.

Sprinting ahead of the crowd, Zacchaeus scrambled up a sycamore tree. And that's when he saw him.

That's him? That's Jesus? Zacchaeus wasn't impressed with his looks. But he was fascinated by how hurting people were drawn to him. A man with stumps where legs used to be, scooting on a cardboard sled, reached out a pathetically deformed hand, trying to touch him. A boy's head swiveled on his scrawny neck, revealing empty sockets where eyes should have been. A woman hysterically howled about her dying daughter. For each he had a tender touch and a compassionate word.

Suddenly Jesus stopped. His head turned, tilted, and his penetrating eyes focused on Zacchaeus.

Matthew edged next to Jesus and whispered, "Master, that's . . ."

"I know," said Jesus, "that's Zacchaeus. We're having lunch with him today."

That grabbed a dozen men's undivided attention! Eyes widened. Jaws dropped.

"We're what?!!"

"Not me, pal."

"I'm outa' here."

"Color me gone."

"Zacchaeus, come down," Jesus said, "I'm going home with you."

"He's going home with *him?*" a scribe sneered. *"What business does he have getting cozy with this crook?"* (Luke 19:7 MSG). Hosannas suddenly turned into hostility.

Draping his arm around Zacchaeus' shoulder, Jesus escorted his newfound friend through the mob.

The next few hours are fuzzy. We don't know what Jesus and Zacchaeus talked about. But we do know the outcome.

"Lord," said Zacchaeus, "I've made a decision. I'm going to give half of all that I have to charity." Big deal! Half of a gazillion is still a bundle. "And . . ." He paused, his eyes taking in the extravagantly furnished room and the impeccably manicured grounds. "And," he continued, "I'm going to make things right with those I've cheated. I am going to give them back four times what I took from them."

Goodbye, ledger! Now Zacchaeus will be able to keep books on the back of an envelope.

Jesus smiled. "This, my friend," he said, thumping the well-worn ledger, "is temporary. This," he said, tapping Zacchaeus on the chest, "this is eternal."

When Zacchaeus' alarm rang that morning, he had awakened to another depressing day in a long string of depressing days. Same old garbage. Stiff a few honest people. Stuff a few dishonest bucks in his pocket. Face off with servants who hated him almost as much as he hated himself. Return home to eat alone. Talk to the walls. Curse into his pillow.

When the lady we met in the last chapter was awakened by rude churchmen crashing through her door, she knew it was going to be a rough day. So what? She had grown used to rough days. Today would only be another episode in her Life Is Lousy existence.

A dismal day for both it seemed. But Jesus had different plans. This was the day he would intersect their paths and change their lives.

Maybe you woke up this morning to a rotten day, too. A marriage gone sour. A business gone south. A child gone bad. A heart gone bitter. Life has done a number on you. You're hurt. Angry. Frustrated. Broke. Lonely. Depressed. Disappointed. Rejected. Stressed. Sick. Scared.

But maybe, just maybe, this is your day. This may be the day he lifts your load. The day he intersects your path at the corner of Miserable and Hopeless, wraps his arm around your shoulder and says, "You don't have to face life alone anymore."

I can almost hear him. Listen!

I'm not telling you that this will be easy. There will be stretches of rough road. But we'll travel together, face whatever comes together. I will never leave you!

"Never?"

"Never!"

Would you like that? Then ask him! Drop your defenses. Get your elbow out of the way. Ask him to come close. To put his arm around your shoulder.

Need help? Here's a little prayer to get you started . . .

Lord, I need your help. I'm tired. I can't make it on my own anymore. I ask you to come close—to let me feel your arm around my shoulder and your peace in my heart.

You take it from there, okay? Take your time. I'll wait for you.

CHAPTER 5

YOU ARE SPECIAL

I t was quite a week. Diana, Princess of Wales, died in Paris. Mother Teresa in Calcutta. And Viktor Frankl in Vienna.

Some other special people died the same week: Joseph Rincon, Loretta Smith, Brian Watson, Rutena Strauss, Edward Washington, and Eleanor Thomas.

Who? Don't recognize those names? Me neither. I randomly lifted them from the obituaries of the Houston Chronicle. Unlike Diana, Teresa, and Viktor, they were unknown, so far as I know, except to family and friends. And to God, who, as the apostle Paul assures us, "has no favorites" (Galatians 2:6 NLT). If that's true, and it is, Loretta Smith was as special to God as Mother Teresa. And so are you.

Don't think so? I'm going to try to convince you. I've got my work cut out for me I know, but I'm going to give it a try.

Do you identify with Charlie Brown of *Peanuts* fame? Charlie Brown is a loser! When he pitches, his team never wins. When he represents his class in the spelling bee, they're eliminated in the first round. Because Charlie Brown is a loser!

That's me! you yelp.

You dreamed of growing to greatness, but you're stuck in the muck of mediocrity. You thought you would soar to the sky, but you haven't gotten off the ground. God knows you've tried, but you're high-centered on average. Or less.

Those profuse predictions your classmates wrote in your high school yearbook haven't happened. They couldn't drag you to a class reunion.

You thought you would have a top-floor corner office, a smashingly stylish spouse, and high-performance kids. But you haven't even reached Assistant-to-the-Assistant-to-the-Vice President, and your office is the corner of the locker room. Your spouse isn't exactly poster material, and you don't sport a bumper sticker saying, *My Child Is an Honor Student at Wahoo Elementary.* Your house is three thousand square feet and two garages shy of your dream home. You are neither driving with distinction nor dressing for success. You've missed these *I've Arrived* prizes by a country mile, and you have the self-image of oatmeal.

You're a loser!

Or maybe you *have* achieved success. You have a trophy spouse. Your kids make straight-A's and have straight teeth. You live in the right neighborhood and your Mercedes is paid for.

And you're miserable!

You have all the trappings of success—the toys, but not the joys. If you could, you would change your name, sneak off to Tahiti, and start fresh. No one else may know, but you do . . .

You're a loser!

How am I doing so far? Feeling better? No?

Okay, let me try again. How about this?

Five sparrows are sold for only two pennies, and God does not forget any of them. But God even knows how many hairs you have on your head. . . . You are worth much more than many sparrows (Luke 12:6-7 ncv).

That's *God's* evaluation of you. He doesn't forget a half-a-cent sparrow, and you're worth more than a tree full of sparrows to him. God forget you? Not a chance!

He knows everything about you. Everything! Your shoe size.

Your favorite food. What you like—and hate—about your job. The color of your eyes. The shape of your nose. How many hairs you have on your head. Everything! And he likes you a lot.

I saw something yesterday I hadn't seen in years. At the convenience store where I stopped for coffee there was a big jar on the counter, filled with beans. They wanted me to buy a chance to guess how many beans were in the jar. If my guess was closest to the right number, I would win the prize (something like a 4 percent discount on a tour of a purification plant in Gagsville, Iowa).

I didn't buy a chance, but I was intrigued. "How many beans are in that jar?" I wondered. Four thousand? Twenty thousand? I didn't have a clue.

While I was mulling the mystery, someone behind me asked, "How many you think's in there?" I turned and was nose-to-nose with a lady with really big hair. Since I had been pondering this chapter, I had to stifle a chuckle. "I'd take my chances with the beans before I'd gamble on how many hairs are pushing through her scalp," I thought. But God knew exactly—about the beans *and* the hair.

Before you go to bed tonight, look in the mirror. Take a guess at the number of hairs on your head. I bet you couldn't come within a thousand, maybe not five thousand. But God knows.

He knows because he wants to.

Because he is that interested in you.

Because you are that valuable to him.

Because he likes you that much.

He doesn't judge your worth by the silly standards we use to measure each other—your financial status, or your dress size, or by where you live, or by what you drive.

He cares about you because you are his child. Because you are special. A thousand angels couldn't convince him otherwise.

November 7, 1958, was one of the happiest days of my life—the day I held a newborn baby in my arms. My son. When the nurse took him from me to return him to the nursery, I walked across the street to a small restaurant for breakfast. The waitress who took my order was unaware, nonchalant. Even yawned at one point. My world had just changed forever, and she acted like it was just another day. To this day forty-two years later, she doesn't know how special my son is. But I do. And God does.

Most newborns look pretty much alike—ragged, rumpled, and wrinkled. Not a pretty sight. (I'll get letters about this.) I've stood and stared through the nursery window with dozens of proud mamas and papas. It's not a time when truthfulness is appreciated. *"That baby's ugly!"* will lose you a friend, sight in one eye, and maybe a tooth or two.

When I was studying for the ministry, I had a professor who spent a lot of time trying to prepare his class of wannabe preachers for the practical aspects of parish life. Among other things, he coached us on visiting new parents. Especially mothers. "Every mother," he said, "thinks her newborn baby is beautiful. In truth," he intoned, "there's never been a pretty newborn." (He had never had children.)

So what to do? Can you be truthful and keep your friends? Your life? "No problem!" he assured. "When you view the infant, thoughtfully rub your chin, assume an attitude of awe, and say, 'Now *theeere's* a baby!'"

Anyway, here's where I was going with this . . .

God is a proud parent. Your father. When you were born, heads turned in heaven. God looked at you and said, "Isn't she beautiful?" If others yawned and acted like it was just another day, that was their problem. You were—and are—special to him. He's nuts about you. He is always thinking about you (1 Peter 5:7 TLB). Your birthday is circled on his calendar, and your picture is in his wallet. Someday he's going to show you some-thing that'll knock your socks off—"See," he'll say, shoving his hand in your face, "I have tattooed your name upon my palm" (Isaiah 49:16, TLB).

You may have been mistreated, neglected, or rejected by your parents. May have been abused or abandoned by the one who promised to be yours for-better-or-for-worse for life. May have been ignored by your church. May have spent a painful lifetime being put down instead of lifted up. May feel friendless and worthless.

Pull up a chair and let me tell you about Lauri before I close this chapter.

Lauri was in the sixth grade. Her classroom was spic-and-span, because this was the day for end-of-the-year conferences. Parents would be coming to school for a progress report from the teacher, Mrs. Lake. A schedule was on the chalkboard, with 20 minutes assigned for each family.

Lauri's name was last on the list. Mrs. Lake had phoned her parents and sent a reminder letter. But Lauri knew her parents wouldn't be coming. Lauri's father was an alcoholic. Many nights this lonely sixth-grader fell asleep listening to her parents fight. They acted as if she didn't exist.

One-after-another the children were called to the hallway door, where they were greeted with smiles and hugs by proud parents. The door would close, and Lauri would hear the muffled voices of parents, child, and teacher. She imagined how it would feel to have her parents greet her at the door. But she knew they wouldn't be there.

After everyone else's name had been called, Mrs. Lake opened the door and motioned for Lauri. She slipped out into the hallway and sat in a chair across from the teacher. Embarrassed that her parents had not come, she folded her hands and looked at the floor. Moving her chair next to Lauri,

Mrs. Lake lifted the little girl's chin so she could make eye contact.

"First of all," she said, "I want you to know how much I love you." Lauri saw in the teacher's eyes things she had rarely seen: compassion, empathy, tenderness.

"Second," Mrs. Lake continued, "you need to know it is not your fault that your parents are not here today." Again Lauri looked into the teacher's eyes. No one had ever talked to her like this. No one.

"Third," she said, "you deserve a conference whether your parents are here or not. You deserve to hear how well you are doing and how wonderful I think you are."

Then Mrs. Lake held a conference just for Lauri. She showed her her grades. She discussed her papers and projects, praising her efforts and affirming her strengths.

Lauri didn't know exactly when, but at some point she heard the voice of hope in her heart. She realized, for the first time in her life, that she was lovable.[1]

Look at me, dear reader. There are three things I want to say to you. It will only take 18 seconds.

First, I want you to know that God loves you.

Second, I want you to know that you are not to blame for some of the things that have happened in your life—that there are some things you can't control.

Third, I want you to know how wonderful God thinks you are. How special. How very, very special.

CHAPTER 6

A BREAKFAST
BUDDY'S ADVICE

I had just slathered a slab of butter on a biscuit and sliced into a sausage when he sat down beside me at the counter. He was roughly the size of Wyoming. Biceps bulged. Shirt seams strained.

"Hi, Bub!" he bellowed.

"Hi." (My voice was higher-pitched than I remembered it being.)

"Been gettin' any exercise, Bub?" he asked, eyeing my cholesterol-loaded plate.

"A little."

"Need t' keep up with that exercise, Bub."

"Right. I've been intending to get with the program," I said. "Can I ask you a question?"

"Sure, Bub. Shoot!"

"What's the best exercise plan?"

"Any plan'll work, Bub." (That "Bub" was getting to me, but it only took me a nanosecond to decide not to make an issue of it without a tire-tool.)

"Yep! Any plan'll work," he continued. "Just two important things. First, you gotta get started. Not next month. Not next week. Not tomorrow. *Today!*

"Second, you gotta keep at it! Don't skip a day. Once you

start skippin' days you'll quit completely. Know what I mean, Bub?"

Hmmm. The gorilla's got a point, I thought.

I was reminded of that conversation this morning when I was jogging. Cars bordered both sides of Cedar Street for half a block. *Too early for a party. Someone must have died.*

Then I saw the sign—*GARAGE SALE!*

My run-by peek at the merchandise revealed a string of fitness fizzles.

Exercise bike.

Rowing machine.

Treadmill.

Like new.

Someone living at 6718 Cedar is a repetitive starter—and stopper.

Get started! Keep at it! My muscle-bound breakfast buddy gave good advice—advice that should be exercised in more than, well, exercise.

Picture a successful person you know. Anyone will do, just pick one. How did that person achieve such success?

Lucky?

Got the breaks?

Right place at the right time?

Huh uh!

There were two primary ingredients: *initiative and endurance.* Think about it. That person had the guts to start and the grit to keep at it. Am I right?

Get Started

Any *Causes-for-Failure* list will position procrastination close to the top. We fail because instead of beginning, we balk.

There are a couple of flaws that are fatal to success.

Fatal Flaw #1: Waiting for the Right Time

Achievers want what they want enough to go after it when conditions are unfavorable. Good thing too, because favorable conditions rarely come. If you wait for the right time, you'll wait a lifetime.

What do you want to be doing five years from now?

I hope it happens. I also hope you understand that what you will be doing five years from now is being decided now!

Several years ago my number-one son was considering returning to school for some advanced education. "But it would take five years," he groused, "and by that time I would be thirty!"

"Five years from now you'll be thirty whether you go back to school or not!" his younger brother countered. *Pow!*

Now, let me ask again: *What do you want to be doing five years from now?* You're going to be five years older whether or not you go for your goal.

I had lunch yesterday with a friend, a Certified Public Accountant. He told me that on his first job, fresh out of college, he saw secretaries tediously punching in column-after-column of figures from the top row of keys on their typewriters. "This is crazy!" he thought. "One of these days I'm going to find a way to link a keypad to those keyboards."

One of these days! Oh, the things we're going to do *one of these days!*

My friend went on to build an impressive career. And let his dream die.

You're ahead of me, aren't you? Today every full-size computer keyboard includes a keypad. And some guy is sitting on a stash of cash, his reward for connecting keypad to keyboard.

My CPA pal had a great idea. But he didn't act. Lost the game without ever suiting up. I've done that. You too?

Fatal Flaw #2: Fear of Failure

Are you reluctant to try because you're afraid you'll fail? Well, by being too shy to try, you surrender to the same result: failure! *Failure by default.*

Believe me, I know.

When I was in college, there was a girl I wanted to date. She was drop-dead gorgeous. For weeks I thought about little else. But every time I reached for the phone, with my nickel and her number, I broke out in a sweat and broke into a stammer. I never dialed her dorm. Know why? I was afraid she would say, "No way, José."

Would she? Maybe. Maybe not. Suppose she had. I would have been no worse off. Fear got me the same result—*no date!* No date is no date, whether by rejection or default.

You can't get the date without asking for it.

You can't win the race without entering it.

You can't achieve the victory without risking defeat.

André Gide said, *"Man cannot discover new oceans unless he has courage to lose sight of the shore."*

Teddy Roosevelt said it this way:

> Far better it is to dare mighty things, to win glorious triumphs, even though checkered by failure, than to take rank with those poor spirits who neither enjoy much nor suffer much because they live in the gray twilight that knows neither victory nor defeat.

Prefer a sentence from Shakespeare? Here's a good one : *Our doubts are traitors, and make us lose the good we oft might win, by fearing to attempt.*

Success involves risk. Always. You can't steal second base and keep your foot on first.

Keep At It

"My mother," said Dwight Eisenhower, "taught me a lesson I'll never forget, perhaps the greatest lesson I have ever learned."

Here's how it happened. While playing a game of Flinch with his mother and brothers, Dwight got a horrible hand. "I give up. This hand is no good," he whimpered.

Mrs. Eisenhower laid her cards down and fixed her young son with a stinging stare. "Dwight," she said, "this is just a game with your mother and your brothers in your own home, and you've been dealt a bad hand. When you get out into life, the world is going to deal you many a bad hand. When you get a bad hand, just play it out and let God help you, and you'll come out all right."

I hope you haven't been dealt a bad hand, but there's a good chance you have. If not, sooner or later you will be.

If you attempt anything above average, you're going to get knocked down occasionally. Count on it! You're going to be abused and bruised. Count on it! It's a factor in the fight, the tuition for triumph. Every success is stained with the blood of defeat and disfigured by the scars of disappointment.

But remember this: you're never beaten by being knocked down; you're only beaten by failing to get up!

From where I am sitting I can tilt my head up and to the right and read this quotation, which hangs on my office wall:

> Nothing in the world can take the place of persistence. Talent will not; nothing is more common than unsuccessful men with talent. Genius will not; unrewarded genius is almost a proverb. Education will not; the world is full of educated derelicts. Persistence and determination alone are omnipotent.[1]

Looking over my shoulder at bygone years, I see many talented acquaintances who never achieved much. Some never started. Others started, stumbled, and stopped. Now they're shuffling into the sunset, thinking about what might have been, blaming fate for their failure.

The most unproductive person on the planet can produce a good excuse for poor performance . . .

I'm too young.

I'm too old.

I'm victim of a dysfunctional family.

I don't belong to the right group.

I don't know the right people.

I don't have the education.

I don't have the resources.

I don't have the time.

I don't get the breaks.

Baloney! I don't want to be insensitive, but that dog won't hunt! Every successful person has had to overcome one of these obstacles. Most have had to overcome several of them. They are only hurdles, not walls!

Harvard's Dean Briggs said, "It is not native gifts, heredity, luck or the right connections that make for success in life. It is doing whatever we do as best we can."

Doing whatever we do as best we can! That's it! Be the best you can be. Nothing more. Nothing less. Nothing else. Don't measure yourself by the achievements of others, but by how you use *your* abilities.

I'm not suggesting a swelled-headed opinion of yourself. I am proposing a powerful partnership—you and Jesus.

As Ethel Waters said, *"Honey, Jesus don't sponsor no flops."*

Commit everything you do to the Lord. Trust him to help you do it and he will (Psalm 37:5 tlb).

If you have faith . . . nothing will be impossible for you (Matthew 17:20).

CHAPTER 7

PLAY TO WIN

Athletes!
Heroes!
Where I went to high school those words were synonymous. Athletes were heroes—the only heroes—in west Texas high schools.

You may not be interested, but here is my athletic record: *No hits! No runs! One error!*

One error?

That's right. *I didn't play.* Never lettered in any sport. Never played on any team. Never even tried out for one. Not that I didn't want to. I envied athletes. Girls liked jocks. And I liked girls.

But it was evident as early as grade school that I was no athlete. (When I'd get to first base, I would forget to turn left, and wind up at B&B Grocery.)

I was always one of the last to be picked when recess teams were chosen. That hurt, but I told myself it didn't. *Who needs it? It's just a silly game. I don't care if I'm not picked. I'd just as soon sit it out.* It was a lie, but it protected my fragile ego. And I did sit it out. Lots of times.

But the game of life doesn't work that way. You can't sit this one out. You're in the game and you have to play. And since you do, you ought to play to win, don't you think?

It's really not that hard. You can win! Let me tell you how in just one word . . .

Persistence!

That was the conclusion of Napoleon Hill. Mr. Hill spent twenty years studying the lives of 500 of the most successful men in America, up until that time.

"The one indispensable ingredient, the common element in the success stories of all of them, was persistence," he said. "These individuals kept trying even after repeated failures . . . Great success was only won by people who overcame incredible obstacles and great discouragement."

> *I had the happy privilege of analyzing both Mr. Edison and Mr. Ford, year by year, over a long period of years, and therefore, the opportunity to study them at close range, so I speak from actual knowledge when I say that I found no quality save persistence, in either one of them, that even remotely suggested the major source of their stupendous achievements.*[1]

"One of the most common causes of failure is the habit of quitting when one is overtaken by *temporary defeat*," he wrote.[2]

Grantland Rice interviewed Babe Ruth in 1927, after the Yanks had clinched the American League pennant.

"Babe," he asked, "what do you do when you get in a batting slump?"

"I just keep goin' up there and keep swingin' at 'em," Babe replied.

If you want to win, you have to *keep swingin'*. Ty Cobb, arguably the greatest slugger of them all, had a lifetime batting average of only .367. In other words, he struck out six times for every ten times at bat.

It takes courage to step back into the batter's box when you connected with nothing but air the last time you tried. But you can't hit it if you don't strike at it. You miss one hundred percent of the ones you don't swing at.

James J. Corbett, former heavyweight champion, said it well:

When your feet are so tired that you have to shuffle back to the center of the ring, fight one more round. When your arms are so tired that you can hardly lift your hands to come on guard, fight one more round. When your nose is bleeding and your eyes are black and you are so tired you wish your opponent would crack you one on the jaw and put you to sleep, fight one more round—remembering that the man who always fights one more round is never whipped.

I never read that statement without thinking about my good friend Ron Willingham. There is no one I admire more, and no one I am prouder of. Ron's company, *Integrity Systems*, is one of the largest sales-training organizations in the world. His clients include some of the biggest companies in the country. Nearly twenty thousand trainers have been certified to conduct the programs he has written. And more than a million and a half people in 38 countries have graduated from them.

Ron has achieved impressive success. But it hasn't been easy. He has confronted crushing crises. Three times it looked like he was down for the count. I'm not talking about a short-term business reversal, a bad quarter, a bad year. I'm talking about losing it all!

Ron accepts full blame for those defeats. Actually they were unavoidable. All three times, he got caught in the jaws of an economic recession just when the foundation of his business had been poured and the cement wasn't quite dry.

He was decked, but he wouldn't stay down. He struggled to his knees, wobbled to his feet, and started swinging. You see, Ron had one asset that was not for sale and not subject to foreclosure—*persistence!* He is, hands down, the most persistent person I know. He refused to quit.

And he doesn't resent his reversals. Just the opposite—he

73

thanks God for them. He believes they have given him perspective and strength he wouldn't have had otherwise. Here are two of his favorite scriptures:

> *Consider it pure joy . . . whenever you face trials of many kinds, because you know that the testing of your faith develops perseverance (James 1:2-3).*

> *We also rejoice in our sufferings, because we know that suffering produces perseverance; perseverance, character; and character, hope (Romans 5:3-4).*

Learn from Ron Willingham, will you? You may be very close to victory. A little more effort, a little more persistence, and what looks like fatal failure may metamorphose into spectacular success. Keep kicking obstacles out of the way. Develop a stubborn streak, a refuse-to-quit-no-matter-what spirit.

Persistence! It's the tuition for success.

In this chapter, and the previous one, I've been writing about the courage to begin and the character to persist. You understand, don't you, that spiritual success carries the same price tag?

We preachers tell you how terrific the Christian life is. And it is. But we seldom tell you how tough it is. (Some of the sermons I hear and religious books I read wouldn't pass the most elementary test of *Truth In Advertising*.)

Truth: the Christian life is a great life, the greatest. But it's not easy. Even the strongest stumble. That's why so many start, then stop. It demands persistence.

C. S. Lewis wrote about the initial rush of excitement that comes with conversion. It's "quite right," he wrote, "that you should feel that 'something terrific' has happened to you." But, he warned, it's also important to understand that you won't always feel that excitement.

Don't imagine it is all "going to be an exciting adventure from now on." It won't . . . . This is the push to start you off on your first bicycle: you'll be left to do lots of dogged pedaling later on. And no need to feel depressed about it either. It will be good for your spiritual leg muscles.[3]

I have no hidden agenda in this book. My aim is to sell you on Jesus, on the Christian life. But I want you to know what you're buying into. And the price. Otherwise you will quit when the going gets tough. And it will get tough.

The Christian life comes with an *eternal warranty*, but with no guarantee of trouble-free operation in *time*. *"You will have trouble,"* the Bible forewarns (John 16:33).

Ask the apostle Paul. In the New Testament he stands among the best of the bunch. But in a paragraph that will take your breath away and leave you shaking your head, he catalogs the catastrophes he endured: floggings, stonings, shipwrecks, false accusations, sleeplessness, hunger, prison, near-death experiences, and more (2 Corinthians 11:21-28).

As a Christian you will face problems that you can't understand. You will wonder where God is and why he doesn't do something. And I must warn you (I wish I didn't have to) that the most disheartening blows will come from within the church, not from without—from those who should be allies, not adversaries.

Look what happened to Jesus . . .

His best friend questioned the legitimacy of his ministry (Matthew 11:2-3).

An insider double-crossed him (Matthew 26:47-49).

His most vocal supporter in private denied him in public. (Matthew 26:69-74).

Jealous church leaders vilified him, saying he was devil-possessed (Mark 3:22).

Religious rulers falsely accused him, illegally tried him, and stupidly sentenced him (Matthew 26:57-66; 27:11-26).

They mocked him, slapped him, beat him, and spat on him (Matthew 26:67; 27:26-31).

And then they killed him (Matthew 26:36-50).

But neither heartbreaking abandonment by fair-weather friends nor torturous treatment by death-dealing enemies diverted him. He had a mission, and he refused to quit until it was accomplished.

He took their worst so he could give you God's best.

If you haven't surrendered your life to him, I hope you will. And if you have, I hope you will stay on the track until the race is finished. Don't quit. When your legs turn to jelly and your lungs scream for mercy, keep running.

When you quit, you're beat. Blame it on your background, circumstances, other people ... whatever. You still lose.

But you're not beat until you quit. *So persist!*

If you do, you will win. *You . . . will . . . win!* You may have lagged in the last lap, but you will win the race, because God helps those who refuse to quit.

He will never leave you!

Never?

Never!

We are perplexed because we don't know why things happen as they do, but we don't give up and quit . . . We get knocked down, but we get up again and keep going . . . we never give up (2 Corinthians 4:8-9, 16 tlb).

. . . run with perseverance the race . . . (Hebrews 12:1).

CHAPTER 8

FIGHT TO THE FINISH

Sparky. That's what his playmates called him when he was a little boy. Sparky—after a comic strip horse named Sparkplug.

School was the pits for Sparky. On his first try at eighth grade he failed every subject. *Every* subject!

High school didn't get much better. He flunked physics. And algebra. And Latin. English, too.

Sparky was socially shunned. His classmates avoided him. Especially girls. In high school he never had a date. Not one. Never even asked a girl for a date. Not once. He was afraid of being turned down.

Sparky was a loser. He knew it. His classmates knew it. Everyone knew it.

The only thing Sparky was good at was art. He had a flair for drawing, and he was proud of his work. In his senior year he submitted some cartoons to the editor of his school yearbook. They were rejected. That hurt.

But Sparky didn't let that snub stop him. He was doggedly determined to become a professional artist. So he wrote a letter to Walt Disney Studios applying for a job as a cartoonist. And here came a form letter, requesting samples of his work.

Sparky worked hard on that assignment. A job with Disney

would be impressive, and there were dozens of doubters to impress. He mailed his drawings to Disney, and waited. And waited . . . and waited . . . and . . .

Finally a reply came. He didn't get the job.

That hurt too. But his mind was set. He knew he had talent, even if others didn't recognize it.

Know what he did? He wrote his autobiography—*in cartoons*. He described his childhood—the little boy loser, the chronic underachiever—in a cartoon character that the whole world now knows. For the boy who failed every course in the eighth grade, the young artist whose work was rejected by Disney and by the editor of his high school yearbook was "Sparky" Charles Monroe Schulz. Yes, *the* Charles Schulz! The artist who created the *Peanuts* comic strip and the little cartoon boy whose kite would never fly—CHARLIE BROWN.

Wouldn't you love to have been a fly on the wall at Sparky's class reunion? Me, too. I bet he wouldn't be turned down for a date to that dance. And as for the editor of the yearbook, and the other classmates who rejected him? Ha!

Here's another story of courage I think you'll like.

Jack grew up with my sons. He spent a lot of time at our house. He was, and is, one of my favorites. Bright, humorous, courteous—and courageous!

Jack knew early on what he wanted to be when he grew up. He wanted to be a doctor. He hit the books hard, and on graduation from college he was accepted into medical school.

But trouble was lurking in the shadows. Midway in the first semester Jack developed an eye infection that became so severe he had to drop out of school. The following year he returned to classes. But his vision quickly deteriorated, and he had to undergo an emergency cornea transplant.

Give up? No way!

May I, with delight and pride, introduce you to my courageous young friend? Shake hands with *Dr. Jack Dyer, M.D.*

When I think of courage, I usually think of the spectacular. Don't you? Like the daring rescue of a child from a burning building. Or parachuting into enemy territory. Or detonating a bomb in the Empire State building. S.W.A.T. type courage!

Or the kind of courage demonstrated by Sparky or Jack.

But courage isn't always so dramatic. Lots of unknown people walk tall through excruciating experiences. *"Quiet Courage"* someone called it.

Charles Swindoll describes it well:

> *Courage is not limited to the battlefield or the Indianapolis 500 or bravely catching a thief in your house. The real tests of courage are much deeper and much quieter. They are the inner tests, like remaining faithful when nobody's looking, like enduring pain when the room is empty, like standing alone when you're misunderstood.*

Swindoll's fine line—*enduring pain when the room is empty*—describes some of the most courageous people on the planet. People who hang in there with a decline-to-whine attitude when they know things aren't likely to get any better.

Nita Short introduces us to some people of *Quiet Courage* whom she met during her chaplaincy at the Texas Medical Center.[1]

The mother who sits day after day caring for her brain-damaged daughter who can't move or talk.

The young man who is terrified of needles, but gives blood so that his father can live.

The young lady who has been diagnosed with Multiple Sclerosis—who doesn't run from the reality but comes to the hospital to help other MS patients.

The wife who sits day after day, week after week, watching her husband go through the suffering of cancer treatment. She is hollow-eyed from lack of sleep, yet she is there encouraging and cheering on her husband.

The old man who has no living relatives to give comfort, who endures his pain alone.

And then there is your story!

I don't know that story, but I have a feeling that it's punctuated with pain. Through the eyes of others it may appear that everything is going your way, that you're living on the sunny side of the hedge. But they don't know the battles you're fighting, the grief you wrestle with alone. Fear. Loneliness. Anxiety. Fill in the blank.

It's tough, and more than once you have been tempted to give up. But you didn't—and you won't—because you have courage.

There is one more type of courage that I want to talk about before I sign off on this chapter—*the courage to come back.* (I must warn you, this isn't for sissies.)

Let's eavesdrop on a conversation between Jesus and Simon Peter (you can find it in Luke 22:31-34).

"Simon! Listen! Satan is going to test you!"

Jesus knew that Satan was going to win the first round in the fight. Knew that Peter was going to kiss the canvas.

Peter didn't buy it. *"Lord, I am ready to go to prison with you and to die with you!"* he babbled.

Jesus knew better. *"I tell you, Peter,"* Jesus said, *"the rooster will not crow tonight until you have said three times that you do not know me."*

"I will never say that, even if I have to die with you!" Peter snorted (Mark 14:31 TEV).

But he did of course. After Jesus' arrest, Peter kept his distance. But he botched it—he didn't keep a *safe* distance. One-after-another, three people pointed at him and said, "He was with Jesus!" And three times he said, "Huh uh, not me. I don't even know him" (see Luke 22:54-62).

Peter's biceps bulged from decades of grappling with heavy fishing nets. His hands were hardened with calluses from the oars and burn marks from the ropes. Yet he couldn't look a wisp of a servant girl in the eye and admit his friendship with Jesus.

He didn't intend to deny Jesus. He really didn't. He was just lying low because he was scared senseless. He couldn't hear anything but three rapid-fire threats and the pounding of his own heart. And his courage collapsed.

Satan won that round. Jesus knew that he would. He knew something else too. Listen . . .

"Simon! Satan is going to test you!" Then he said, *"When you turn back to me . . . strengthen your brothers."*

Did you catch that? *"When you turn back to me!"* Not *if*, but *when!* He knew that Peter would bounce back.

It took a lot of courage. Peter was crushed by his cowardice. And embarrassed. Most people would have assumed an alias and hit the road. How could he face his comrades of the past three years? Not easy. After all, just two days earlier he had boasted of his strength and hinted at their weakness. *"I will never leave you, even though all the rest do!"* he had said to Jesus (Mark 14:29 TEV).

Now he had to eat crow. Had to look them in the eye and say, "I owe you an apology. I thought I was stronger than you. I wasn't. I should have been looking at myself, but I had my eye on you. I'm sorry."

Jesus believed in Peter. He knew he would deny him, but he also knew he would turn back to him. Peter has two letters in the New Testament because he had the courage to come back—because he refused to live in the shadow of his failure. And he was transformed from one who denied with an oath into one who witnessed with a passion.

Jesus believes in you, too.

I know, you've had your moments of weakness and failure. At one time or another, in one way or another, all of us have denied him. But you can come back, if you have the courage. Regardless of the promises you have broken and the vows you have neglected, he is ready—eager—to receive you back.

You may have lost a round or two, but the fight isn't over. You're not in this alone. Jesus is in your corner, and he isn't about to throw in the towel. He believes you're a champ.

He will never give up on you!

Never?

Never!

CHAPTER 9

THE HARDEST QUESTION

Adam Scott had just finished law school and signed on with a prestigious Los Angeles firm. Those who knew him well were eager to watch his career unfold. He would climb fast and go far, they were certain of that. His personality, talent, sensitivity, and commitment destined him to greatness. "He will be Governor some day," a friend predicted.

It wasn't to be. On October 23, 1993, this bright, dynamic, lovable27-year-old was senselessly shot to death. A needless, devastating loss.

Dr. Jack Scott, Adam's father, has had a distinguished career as a preacher, professor, college president, politician, and dad. Lacreta, Adam's mother, has excelled as a teacher, lecturer, and mom. I have known them both since college days, and greatly admire their unusual abilities and uncommon accomplishments.

More than that, I respect them because success hasn't changed them and adversity hasn't embittered them. They were abruptly, brutally tested by the death of their son. Bruised and broken, they had to continue to live when it would have been easier to die. But they have courageously coped with the tragedy, and been role models for all of us who are pulverized by pain.

Jack and Lacreta love God and have fervent faith. A couple of God's best. Still, in the quiet hours their pain has been excruciating. And a devilish, unanswered question stalks in the shadows . . .

Why?

News spread like a grass fire that Jesus was in town! From every direction people rushed to see him and crushed anything that got in their way. It looked like the doors at Macy's had just swung open on sale day. Bodies crammed into the house where he was staying until every inch was occupied.

Hoping for healing, four men toting a paralytic on a pallet clawed through the crowd. Too late. The place was packed. So they did something that you would get arrested for—they ripped the roof off! Literally. Then they lowered their disabled friend until he was lying right in front of Jesus (Matthew 2:1-4). Not very respectful, but definitely resourceful. Give them that.

This paralyzed man was fortunate to have such friends. They had known him when he was well, and they didn't forget him when he wasn't. Self-sufficiency was past tense for him. Yesterday he could take care of himself. Today he couldn't. Couldn't dress himself, feed himself, bathe himself, brush his teeth, or blow his nose.

I know a man like that. He can't put on his glasses, cut his nails, comb his hair, or scratch his ear. "If you could choose just one thing," I asked him, "what would you most like to do?" His answer surprised—and shamed—me. "More than anything," he said, "I would like to shave myself just one more time."

I hate to shave. Always have. It takes too much time, and it hurts. At least that's the way I felt before my friend knocked the whine out of me. As he dozed off, I tiptoed out of his room.

Pulling the door shut I whispered, "God, I will never complain about shaving again. Never! That's a promise."

May I get personal for a couple of paragraphs?

The story I just told you has paid a personal visit to my house. Walked through my door. Without knocking. Uninvited. And has refused to leave. It has taken up residence in the next room where my wife Alyce lies in bed, paralyzed from the waist down and deteriorating from the waist up. Diagnosed a dozen years ago with multiple sclerosis, she has become progressively disabled. She can't write, walk, roll over in bed—can't do anything for herself.

In these twelve years I have never heard her ask, "Why me?" Not once. I admire her enormously for that. But I must confess that the question has sunk its fangs in me a few times . . . *Why her?*

Deaths of loved ones and disabling ailments are by no means the only problems that prompt a *Why?*

Life is tough. You can't live long without coming eyeball-to-eyeball with agony. Let your mind wander back over the past few days. You, or someone you know, has been bloodied by the blows of trouble. You have sat shaking your head at the horrid stories of the hurting.

Here's my list:

An acquaintance who is facing crushing financial problems and the embarrassing probability of bankruptcy.

A woman who is struggling to survive the procedures of an unwanted—and very nasty—divorce.

A man who is trapped in a miserable marriage.

A mom and dad whose child has broken their hearts.

A friend who is trying to endure with dignity the final stages of an agonizing and apparently futile fight with cancer.

Your story, if I knew it, would probably add a paragraph to this chapter. On any block in any neighborhood there is enough suffering to make your blood freeze. And the question that won't go away is . . .

Why?

God has the power to erase this anguish in a heartbeat. So why doesn't he? My apologies, but if you're asking me, you are asking the wrong person. Or at least at the wrong time. (You should have asked me thirty years ago when I had all the answers.)

There isn't a preacher on the planet who wouldn't trade his diploma for the answer to the *Why?* question, because he hears it a dozen times a month from people who limp through his door. And he doesn't have the answer.

Not only do we not have the answer, we ask the same question. Preachers are supposed to have answers, not questions, right? We're expected to take the mystery out of misfortune, give easy answers to hard questions. But when we face a tough *Why?* we don't have an answer.

That was Job's question, too. *Why?* This good man agonized over his afflictions. He had been unmercifully hammered by undeserved suffering. Digging through the ashes of his crashed-and-burned life, he begged for an explanation. He was angry. He wanted a face-to-face confrontation with God. He ached for an answer. And he finally got it—a confrontation with God, that is.

And what did God say? He plunged into a verbal tour of creation, constellations, lightning, thunderstorms, and wild animals.

But he didn't answer Job's question!

I don't get it, do you? Here was the perfect place for God to explain once-and-for-all the mystery of suffering. Or so it seems to me. With a dozen well-crafted sentences, he could have answered Job's question—and Jack's and Lacreta's, and mine, and yours. But he didn't. Why?

I don't know. But since he didn't, I would be foolish to

repeat the mistake of Job's arrogant advisers and try to do it for him.

Still, God did speak. And his message was clear:

Until you can make the sun rise, or shake the clouds and make it rain, or hurl a lightning bolt, or make a hippopotamus, or tame a crocodile, don't tell me how to run the world! And don't accuse me of injustice! There is a lot you don't know. You are not God, I am God! Remember that! I . . . am . . . God!

I just reread that last paragraph and thought, "Lighten up, Joe, your loose paraphrase paints a portrait of a surly God." So I thumbed over to the book of Job and reread God's actual words (Job 38-41). It's a rough read. He sounds brusque, even sarcastic. Yet, something tells me that his tone wasn't testy, because Job was satisfied.

Satisfied? Yes. Satisfied to let God be God.

And that, I think, is the best we can do—*let God be God*.

I wonder—we all do—why he doesn't answer our *Whys*. But you can hardly find a page in your Bible that doesn't entreat you to just trust him.

He wants you to trust him when you throb with undeserved hurt and unexplained grief. He wants you to trust him even when he is silent.

And sometimes he is silent. Sometimes, for reasons known to him but not to us, he refuses to intervene.

Don't think that you have been singled out for this silent treatment. Jesus experienced it too, and asked the same question that tortures us . . . *Why?*

"My God," he cried from the cross, *"why have you forsaken me?"*

And God was silent. He didn't answer, and he didn't intervene. He couldn't, if we were to be saved. What was happening on the cross *had* to happen, for our benefit. God heard the cry of his Son. You can be sure of that. But he turned away from him, for us . . . turned away to weep, I think.

When you cry *Why?* he may not answer. And he may not intervene. But you can be sure he hears your cry. If it seems that he has turned away from you, he has turned away to weep, I think.

Just trust him. It's a tall order, I know. Easier said than done. But it brings peace when nothing else will.

In an accident in the Sierras, Tim Hansel suffered an injury that has packaged him in a pain-wracked body from that day until this. His body is weak, but his trust is strong. During one of the most difficult days of his life, a friend sent him a plaque with this message:

> Tim,
> Trust me
> I have everything
> under control!
> Jesus[1]

You may hear no answer to your *Why?* Trust him anyway. He really does have everything under control.

CHAPTER 10

HOPE IN HIM

Hope (hōp) v. **1**. To entertain a wish for something with some expectation. **2**. To be confident; trust. To look forward to with confidence of fulfillment; expect with desire.

That's the dictionary definition of hope. Personally, I like this non-dictionary definition better: *To believe good things are going to happen.*

In case you're interested, neurological researchers say that the left side of your brain is cognitive.

What does that mean? Well, it means that the left side of your brain sifts through puzzles of logic. If it's working right, it puts all the pieces in the proper places: round pegs in round holes, square pegs in square holes. Never square pegs in round holes. It makes decisions based on facts, nothing but facts.

And the right side of the brain? That's the artistic and intuitive side, where decisions are made on the basis of instincts, hunches, hopes, dreams.

Have you noticed that we tend to trust people who make

decisions with the logical left side of the brain, people who rely only on facts? And that we distrust dreamers?

That's odd. That we distrust dreamers, I mean. Because most of the things we depend on day-in-and-day-out were conceived by dreamers: churches and schools, books and businesses, cars and computers. You name it, chances are it originated with a dreamer.

If we demand that decisions be made only on the basis of known facts, we are imprisoned by the past and can't reach beyond what has already been discovered. But when we dare to dream, we leap into the exciting world of hope, of endless possibility!

Over a hundred years ago Jules Verne, the French novelist, spun nail-biting tales about submarines that traveled under the polar ice cap, and spaceships that flew to the moon. His stories were pure fantasy, of course. They were entrancingly entertaining, but no one took them seriously.

Voilà! Verne's fantasies have long since become fact. It's old stuff now. Submarines? Boring. Rocket launches? Yawn. We're impressed with the technology, but keep it off of TV! Don't mess with me by preempting my programs. *"We interrupt this program to bring you . . ."* I don't wanna hear it!

Cars. Television. Microwaves. Computers. These and a million other marvels would be non-existent except for the imagination of the Jules Vernes of the world. It was their dreams that nudged left-brained scientists to build the conveniences we can't live without. Scientists and engineers can crunch the numbers and put the pieces together, but it takes the vision of a Verne to trigger the process.

In the 1960's social psychologist Robert Rosenthal began researching what he called *Experimenter Bias*. He wondered if an experimenter's bias affected how he approached and performed an experiment. And if so, did that in turn affect the results? In other words, did expectations influence outcome?

One of Rosenthal's projects involved giving a group of elementary school children a standard IQ test. He didn't grade the tests, only pretended to. He *randomly* selected twenty percent of those children and told their teachers that they were intellectually superior to the other students in their classes. "You can expect exceptional academic performance and unusual intellectual gains from these students during the school year," he told them.

Guess what! These kids significantly outperformed the other children. Surprised? Of course not. The teachers' expectations were communicated to those children, and they worked to live up to them.

It's a sword that cuts both ways. For instance, I have an acquaintance who got in his son's face every time he brought home a less-than-perfect report card. "You little punk!" he would shout, "you'll wind up in prison!" And sure enough, that boy is now fulfilling his dad's expectations as a guest of the government.

In Chapter 3 we talked about the power of affirmation—how we tend to live up to the expectations of others. We also live up to the expectations we have for ourselves. Putting yourself down as incompetent, incapable, ineffective, and inept is a sure way to program yourself for failure.

But when you feel good about yourself, believe in yourself, and have high hopes and eager expectations, forces are set in motion to fulfill those hopes and expectations.

Don't mark off as a foolish fanatic the person who says . . .

If you can picture it, you can possess it.

If you can conceive it, you can achieve it.

Thomas Edison has been called *the man who invented the twentieth century.* If I asked you to tell me about old Thomas, I bet I know the first thing you would say: "He invented the light bulb." No doubt this 1879 invention put his name in the encyclopedia.

Know what? That bulb wasn't worth much. It was too expensive, out of reach for all but the rich. Besides, it didn't produce much light, and it didn't last long. It had three strikes against it when it came off the workbench.

Enter William David Coolidge. Coolidge spent seven years trying to find a filament that would make Edison's light bulb useable. At the time, tungsten was the only known element that could be used as a filament. But metallurgical scientists unanimously and authoritatively said that tungsten was not sufficiently malleable. "It will never work!" they sniffed.

Coolidge continued experimenting anyway, and—you guessed it—he made it work. When he was asked how he succeeded when the experts said he couldn't, he replied, "It was because I am not a metallurgist. Had I been a metallurgist, I would have known that it was impossible."

What am I saying to you? Trust your dreams! And act on them! Don't slink into a back seat because you're short on training, credentials, or experience. Keep plugging away at your hopes. To borrow Winston Churchill's famous five-word speech . . . *"Never, never, never give up!"*

"But Joe, it isn't easy to have hope!" you protest.

And you're absolutely right, of course. Hundreds of hope-smashing experiences assault us. Life isn't easy. Not always fair either.

In the last chapter we visited Job. Do you mind if we revisit him in this one?

Job is a case study in *unfair*. He invested years building a storybook life. And in one soul-shattering day lost it all—plunged from prosperity to poverty, from happiness to heartache. *In just one day!*

It started with a gang of rustlers murdering his hired hands and stealing his livestock.

On the heels of that, his children—all ten of them—were

killed in a tornado. One day, one family, ten graves.

And that wasn't all. Before the sun set, Job came down with shingles. Actually it was worse than that. (Excuse me, this isn't dinner table talk.) Nasty sores broke out all over his body, from feet to scalp. They festered and ruptured, and worms bred in his putrefying flesh.

Adding to his agony, his wife badgered him and his friends blamed him.

Venting his misery, he said that he wished he had never been born, and begged God to let him die. Who could blame him? (Except his self-righteous so-called friends?)

"Who can see any hope for me?" he moaned.

Then he answered his own question: *"I will hope in him!"* He was angry with God, but he still trusted him. And after awhile his hope was rewarded:

> . . . *the Lord made him prosperous again and gave him twice as much as he had before . . . The Lord blessed the latter part of Job's life more than the first (Job 42:10,12).*

Bad things do happen to good people. Maybe to you. I wish I could explain it and make your hurt go away. I can't. But don't give up hope! I know, that's easy to say and hard to do. I wouldn't dare diagnose your pain as anything less than the terrible torment that it is. But hope is your only chance for survival. It's your grip on God. If you are the child of an all-powerful, ever-present God, you have reason to hope, because he is in control.

That's the way Joseph saw it.

Joseph's jealous brothers sold him into slavery for a shabby sack of silver. When they came face-to-face with him years later on foreign turf, he said, *"It was not you who sent me here, but God"* (Genesis 45:8).

Joseph believed that God could—and would—bring good out of bad. And he was right, of course.

*We know that in **all things** God works for the good of those who love him (Romans 8:28, emphasis mine).*

Here's another example of how hope gives you the edge.

The book of Habakkuk gets its name from a usually-ignored prophet. (No wonder. No one could say his name without laughing. I'd sue my parents if they had named me Habakkuk.)

Anyway, Habakkuk is a short little book just a few pages from the end of the Old Testament. Let's blow the dust off of it and read a few lines.

Even though the fig trees have no blossoms, and there are no grapes on the vine; even though the olive crop fails, and the fields lie empty and barren; even though the flocks die in the fields, and the cattle barns are empty, yet I will rejoice in the Lord! I will be joyful in the God of my salvation (3:17-18 NLT).

That's grim reading, until you get to the last seventeen words. Habakkuk lived in horribly hard times. But he refused to surrender his hope, his trust in God. God-trusting hope can turn your calamity into tranquility.

Paul put in a good word for hope too:

We can rejoice when we run into problems and trials for we know that they are good for us—they help us learn to be patient. And patience develops strength of character in us and helps us trust God more each time we use it until finally our hope and faith are strong and steady (Romans 5:3-5 TLB).

One more thing before I close this chapter.

God had something big, very big, in mind when he spoke of hope. He didn't promise exemption from affliction, or an easy life. But he did promise resurrection, and eternal life:

In his great mercy he has given us new birth into a living hope through the resurrection of Jesus Christ from the dead, and into an inheritance that can never perish, spoil, or fade (1 Peter 1:3-4).

As we agreed earlier, it's hard to hope. Hard, but not impossible. Because of Jesus, hope is within reach.

Maybe you're a little down-and-out, having a hard time living today and facing tomorrow, plagued by your past or your pain.

Let Jesus help. He wants to. He can. He will.

Hope in him.

CHAPTER 11

JUST BELIEVE

J airus and his wife sat holding hands. In silence. Stunned. His face was pinched and pasty. She stared into space, eyes glazed. Friends stood in clusters nearby fidgeting uncomfortably, wanting to say something but unable to find appropriate words.

Slipping out of the bedroom, the doctor pulled the door shut behind him. He walked toward them with tired, heavy steps, his face drained and drawn. He'd had to break this news a hundred times, but it never got any easier. *Words are clumsy tools to work with at a time like this,* he thought caustically, *like a jeweler trying to repair a watch with a crowbar.*

"I'm sorry . . ." he began. The words stuck in his throat. *Is that all I can say? I'm sorry? Sorry words, I say. Sorry, stinking words!*

"Isn't there anything we can do, somewhere we can take her?" Jairus pleaded.

The doctor shook his head. "I've consulted the most highly-respected specialists. There's no treatment."

"How long?"

"Couple of hours . . . maybe less."

Jairus's hand trembled as he brushed away a tear. Incoherent scraps of thought without beginning or end swirled

105

in his fevered mind. He was frantically reaching out for God, and grabbing fistfuls of air.

Dear God, why?! he thought bitterly. *I've devoted my whole life to you. She's only twelve . . . twelve . . . do you hear me? Only twelve years old! A baby. Why her? Why us?!! If you have to flex your cosmic muscles and decrease the population by one today take me, not her!!* He was confused. Hurt. Angry.

Jairus's wife buried her face in her hands. Her thin body convulsed with uncontrollable sobs. Taking her in his arms, Jairus said, "I'll be back. I'm going to find that teacher."

The Chairman of Jairus' Board gulped. "Brother Jairus," he said, grabbing his arm, "don't! I know how hard this is for you, but don't do this!"

"I have to."

"But he can't help! You know that. Don't do it!"

"I have to."

"You'll be sacrificing your reputation, your career, everything you've worked for."

"I know."

Jairus was one of the city's best-known citizens—Senior Minister of its biggest church, president of the Rotary Club, past chairman of the United Way.

And one of the most visible and vocal preachers in the brotherhood. Defender of truth. Guardian of orthodoxy. Fearless. Tough as nails. His sermon last Sunday was a scorcher. He had scalded this itinerant renegade teacher. "A despicable fake faith-healer, preying on the guilt and hysteria of sick people!" he hollered. "A fly-by-night opportunist! An egomaniac! A heretic!" he screamed.

But that was then. This was now. And *now* his daughter was dying.

Bone-chilling, blood freezing tragedy has a way of moderating one's view.

If there is a chance—however slight—that he can help . . . Is there? Can he? The doctor says there's no hope. Maybe not, but . . .

His tortured brain replayed the stomach-churning picture of his little girl's dainty, fragile body being invaded by piercing needles and ghastly tubes.

His legs were numb, threatening to collapse under him, but he kept elbowing and stumbling his way through the crowd. Finally he saw him.

Jesus' eyes were darting from face to face, as if he was looking for someone. When he spotted Jairus, his clear, dark eyes stopped and locked into his. Jairus had never seen such penetrating eyes, eyes that communicated so much. Jesus edged through the crowd to meet him. He seemed to know why he was here, even before a word was spoken.

"My little girl is dying. I . . . I need help," said Jairus.

"Take me to her."

Their exit was interrupted by four rude messengers, bulldozing through the mob. The moon-faced fop that reached Jairus first was gasping for breath. "Your daughter is dead!" he wheezed. "There's no need to bother the teacher now." He fixed Jesus with a contemptuous *what-do-you-have-to-say-to-that?* smirk.

Ignoring the intrusion, Jesus put his hands on Jairus's sagging shoulders, looked deeply into his eyes, and said, *"Don't be afraid . . . just believe."*

A large crowd had gathered at the parsonage—parishioners, friends, community brass. Women wept openly. Macho men turned away, pawing their eyes with callused knuckles.

"Don't cry," Jesus said, "the child isn't dead, she's just sleeping."

That set them off . . .

"Sleeping? Are you nuts?"

"What's the matter with you, don't you have any respect?"

"I ought to twist your nose off!"

Exhausted, but instinctively proper, Jairus introduced Jesus to his wife. She nodded, biting a trembling lip. "Oh, my baby, my precious baby," she sobbed. "Please, God, not my baby!"

Jesus gently took her arm and whispered, "Let's go in and see her."

Walking to the bedside, he took the child's cold, delicate hand in his and said softly, "Get up, little girl."

Her eyelids fluttered. Then her eyes opened. Big as saucers. Bright as stars. Swinging her feet off the bed, she smiled, and skipped across the room into the arms of her half-crying, half-laughing parents.

"Better get her something to eat," Jesus said. "She's probably starving."[1]

Belief came hard for Jairus, but it came. And it made all the difference—the difference between death and life!

The Marquis of Lossie was dying. He sent for the devout schoolmaster, Mr. Graham.

"Are you satisfied with yourself, my lord?" asked the schoolmaster.

"No, by God!"

"You would like to be better?"

"Yes; but how is a poor devil to get out of this infernal scrape?"

"Keep the commandments!"

"That's it, of course; but there's no time!"

"If there were but time to draw another breath, there would be time to begin!"

"How am I to begin? Which am I to begin with?"

"There is one commandment which includes all the rest!"

"Which is that?"

"Believe on the Lord Jesus Christ and thou shalt be saved!"[2]

Thomas Chalmers, the nineteenth century Scottish preacher, agreed. In a letter to his brother he wrote:

> I am now most thoroughly of the opinion that on the system of *"Do this and live!"* no peace can ever be attained. It is *"Believe on the Lord Jesus Christ and thou shalt be saved!"* When this belief enters the heart, joy and confidence enter along with it!

Believe! said the schoolmaster.

Believe! said Thomas Chalmers.

What did they mean? They meant that the person (Jesus) must precede the precepts and the prohibitions. That faith must come first, always first. That everything else will fall into place if you really believe.

What about the commandments? Believe, and all the King's horses and all the King's men couldn't keep you from keeping his commandments (see John 14:15).

What about works? Believe, and works are sure to follow (see James 2:18).

Faith comes first—the foundation upon which all else is built. A doctrine of salvation by *works* will drive you to double your effort and work twice as hard. A doctrine of salvation by *faith* will empower you to work twice as hard with half the effort.

Believe! This is where it all begins and ends.

For the gospel reveals how God puts people right with himself: it is through faith from beginning to end. As the scripture says, "The person who is put right with God through faith shall live" (Romans 1:17 TEV).

He is reaching out to you, just as he did to that distraught dad, saying, *"Just believe!"*

All things are possible for the one who believes (Mark 9:23 NCV).

CHAPTER 12

DON'T YOU REMEMBER?

I t had happened 150 years ago, but our guide told the story so masterfully that you'd have sworn she had been there. Her monologue was magnificent. I was mesmerized as she crescendoed toward the finale of a perfect presentation. Punching a hole in the air with her index finger she trumpeted, *"Remember, what happened here was the most important event in history!!!"*

Whoa!

Now understand that I am a native Texan. And that we were in San Antonio. At the Alamo. A site that memorializes a colorful and important chapter in Texas lore.

But *the most important event in history?* That's carrying *"Remember the Alamo!"* a pep-rally past reality.

There are more important things to remember.

May I mention a few?

Remember What God Wants

He wants you to trust him—to have faith.

You can hardly say faith without saying Abraham. Abraham was 75 years old when God abruptly notified him that he was being transferred—omitting little details such as where he would be going and what he would be doing.

Leave your country, your people . . . and go to the land I will show you (Genesis 12:1).

Know what I would have said? I would have said: "Excuse me? You mean just pack my stuff—leave Ur, my hometown, and just go? Destination and assignment unknown?"

That's right, I would have asked those questions before I packed the first pair of socks! But Abraham didn't. He grabbed his bags and headed for the door.

I can almost hear the conversation ...

"Going on vacation, Abraham?"

"Nope. Moving."

"You're leaving Ur?"

"Yep."

"Where you going?"

"Er-r-r-r."

"Ur? You're in Ur. You said you were moving. Where to?"

"Er-r-r-r."

He didn't have a clue.

Abraham trusted God, and when God told him to leave home and go far away to another land . . . he went, not even knowing where he was going (Hebrews 11:8 TLB).

And God wasn't finished. He proceeded to make a promise that was an even bigger trust-tester:

I will give you many descendants, and they will become a great nation (Genesis 12:2 TEV).

Get real! Abraham didn't have any children. Descendants without kids? *Many* descendants? How do you get *many* when you don't have *any*?

Just so Abraham wouldn't think that his hearing was going, God said it again:

Look at the sky and try to count the stars; you will have as many descendants as that (Genesis 15:5, TEV).

Then what? Two and a half decades of baffling silence, that's what.

Abraham believed anyhow. A guy who's got the guts to leave Ur for Er-r-r-r has a five-star faith.

Five years after God made that promise they threw Abraham's eightieth birthday bash. No child.

Eighty-five. No child.

Ninety. No child.

Ninety-five. No child.

Ninety-nine!! Give it up, Abraham. There ain't gonna be no tot in your tent.

"Yes there is! God said so!"

Come on! Sarah was 90, and infertile. And Abraham was pushing a hundred. The Hebrew writer summed it up in a single sentence—they were *"as good as dead"* (Hebrews 11:12). It was inconceivable (no pun intended) that they would have a child. Abraham passing out cigars at a hundred? Sarah fixing formula at 90? What a knee-slapper.

God dangled this promise in front of Abraham and Sarah, filled their hearts with hope, and then sat on his hands and watched them totter into old age.

What was he doing? What did he want?

Faith. He wanted faith. Wanted Abraham to believe even when it wasn't reasonable. Abraham did. And God kept his promise. Those who hung around long enough saw Abraham playing *this-little-piggy-went-to-market* with his son.

Now there's a great big, industrial-strength faith for you.

You see, there is a faith that you can respond to with action. Then there's a more demanding faith—a faith that you can't answer with action, only with trust.

When God told Abraham to pack and leave home, there

was something he could do. He could pack and leave home. Not without a lump in his throat, but he could do it.

But when God told Abraham that he was going to have a son, there was nothing he could do. He and Sarah had been trying to have a baby since they were newlyweds. Here was a promise that Abraham just had to accept, totally trusting God for its fulfillment.

You face off with faith at these two levels, too.

If you feel God calling you to a mission field, there is something you can do. You can pack and go.

If you feel God calling you to make a financial gift, there is something you can do. You can get out your check book.

If you feel God calling you to stand above the muck of gossip or dishonesty, there is something you can do. You can refuse to participate.

But it's faith of a different dimension when your hands are tied, when there is nothing you can do.

When the cancer has spread and the doctors say there's nothing more they can do, there is nothing you can do but trust him.

When your loved one is dying and you have exhausted every possible source of help, there is nothing you can do but trust him.

When you have given a lifetime of loyalty to your company and you get your pink slip, and you're too old to be an attractive candidate for another job, and you have no idea how you're going to make ends meet, there is nothing you can do but trust him.

When your heart is breaking and your tears are splashing on the divorce papers, there is nothing you can do but trust him.

But God honors the faith that honors him, the faith that trusts him when everything is fuzzy, when you can't see for the fog.

DON'T YOU REMEMBER

What is faith? It is the confident assurance that something we want is going to happen. It is the certainty that what we hope for is waiting for us, even though we cannot see it up ahead (Hebrews 11:1 TLB).

Another thing. Faith is fortified by a peek at the past. So . . .

Remember What God Has Done

With ten eye-popping plagues God rattled Pharaoh until he released his grip his brick-making Hebrew slaves. And even then, God's miraculous care for his people was just beginning. In the weeks that followed the Israelites watched as God opened a way for them through the Red Sea, poured out fresh drinking water for them and their herds out of a rock, turned back an attack by an army of angry nomads, and covered the ground morning after morning with free food called manna. Everything Israel needed God supplied.

Then one day God summoned Moses to Sinai for a 40-day crash course in the law. That old mountain belched thunder and lightning and smoke, and scared the sap out of everybody. (Fear has a way of provoking promises.) *"We will do everything the Lord has said,"* the people promised (Exodus 19:8).

Right! They flipped just one page of the calendar before violating their vow. One month and ten days after making that promise they came whining to Aaron:

We do not know what has happened to Moses . . . so make us a god to lead us (Exodus 32:1 TEV).

And weak-kneed Aaron crumbled. When Moses came down from the mountain, he found them worshiping a blood-less, breathless, brainless bovine made out of 14-carat earrings.

It took them just 40 days to forget everything God had been doing for them for years.

117

But cut them a little slack. It had been a tough trek in a *"vast and dreadful desert . . . with venomous snakes and scorpions"* (Deuteronomy 8:15). They would do better when they got to the Promised Land, wouldn't they?

Don't count on it. God told Moses:

These people will soon prostitute themselves to the foreign gods of the land they are entering. They will forsake me and break the covenant I made with them . . . I know what they are disposed to do, even before I bring them into the land (Deuteronomy 31:16, 21).

So when Moses gave them the Ten Commandments, he spiked his sermon with these words:

*Remember how the Lord your God led you all the way in the desert these forty years . . . When you have eaten and are satisfied, praise the Lord your God for the good land he has given you. **Be careful that you do not forget** the Lord your God . . . when you eat and are satisfied, when you build fine houses and settle down, and when your herds and flocks grow large and your silver and gold increase and all you have is multiplied, then your heart will become proud and **you will forget** the Lord* (Deuteronomy 8:2, 10-14, emphasis mine).

And sure enough they did!

Do you? Do you forget what God has done?

I do. And that's too bad, because short memory is a sure way to short-circuit faith.

This very day I have been wallowing in the *"poor me"* mud of poor memory. Maybe I'd better tell you about it.

In this morning's mail I received one of those fat, brown, bet-you-can't-look-at-this-without-sweating envelopes—from the Internal Revenue Service. They want to have another look at one of my past tax returns. Hoo boy!

I know what they want—more of my money. Their unpublicized mission-statement is: *You make it, we take it!*

See! It just takes one piece of mail to get me bent out of shape. I get anxious and angry. I sweat and stew. And I forget God's year-after-year-after-year help. He has always taken care of me.

I've seen times when I didn't know how I was going to make the house payment. Times when I couldn't pay the electric bill. Times when I didn't have grocery money. Times when . . . well, you know, you've been there, too.

But God has always come through. Somehow the bills have always been paid. Still, the slightest shortage throws me into a tailspin. Why? Short memory, that's why.

I'm sure you remember the following story, but you may not remember how it ended.

With five loaves of bread and two fish Jesus fed 5,000 families. When the picnic was over, his disciples picked up the leftovers—twelve basketfuls. Three days later, with seven loaves of bread and a short string of fish, he fed 4,000 more. Another seven basketfuls of scraps (Matthew 14:15-21; 15:32-38).

It would be hard to forget an experience like that, wouldn't it?

Not really. By supper time Jesus' disciples were hungry as bears, and just about as congenial. A dozen growling stomachs and grumbling spirits. Hey! didn't anybody bring a basket of fish sticks from the picnics?

If Guinness had been around, these guys would have rated a page in his book—world record for the shortest memory.

Now here is the ending that I said you may not remember. Jesus chided his disgruntled disciples:

> Don't you remember the five loaves for the five thousand, and how many basketfuls you gathered? Or the seven loaves for the four thousand, and how many basketfuls you gathered? (Matthew 16:9-10).

Interpretation: "I just fed 9,000 famished families without breaking a sweat. A snack for a dozen shouldn't be a problem, should it?"

Don't you remember? Good question. For them. For me. Maybe for you.

Don't you remember?

Well, no, to be truthful I don't remember. I don't remember the day when I was strapped for cash to pay the electric bill. Don't even remember the year. It was gut-wrenching at the time, but until I started writing this chapter, I had forgotten about it.

And I don't want to forget it. I really don't. Because faith puts on muscle when you survive the storm and know without a doubt that God got you through it. When there is no other explanation. When you know that you didn't have the knowledge, ability, or resources to make it on your own. When there can be no pride—only grateful acknowledgment that God stepped in.

Lay this book in your lap and think about the disasters in your past for a few minutes, will you? Over the shoulder they don't look too bad do they? Remember what God has done.

One more thing . . .

Remember That God Keeps His Promises

Joshua succeeded Moses as Israel's Commander in Chief. He piloted them to the Promised Land, led them in battle, divided the land among them, and mediated their squabbles. It was a crushing job.

When he was old and tired and about to die, he reminded them that God had made good on all his promises:

You know . . . that not one of all the good promises the Lord your God gave you has failed. Every promise has been fulfilled; not one has failed (Joshua 23:14).

God keeps his promises. Always. Remember that.

When he says *I will never leave you,* he won't.

When he says *I will be with you always,* he will.

When he says *I forgive and forget your sins,* he does.

When he says *I am preparing a place for you where there will be no more tears,* he is.

CHAPTER 13

AN UNFINISHED STORY

She sat at the end of the pew, three rows from the front. Her mind was worlds away.

It had been twenty-four years since she met the man who was responsible for her being here. *Twenty-four years!* She shook her head, and a smile played upon her lips.

Her hair was now flecked with gray. Crow's-feet wrinkles creased the skin at the corners of her eyes. Her back was bowed and her pace was slow, but she was more beautiful than ever. She had a young and happy heart that exploded in a megawatt smile.

She was roused from her reflection by shuffling feet. The preacher had taken his position at the podium. He had a letter he said—from Paul, the apostle—and he wanted to read a paragraph or two. He fished his glasses from his inside coat pocket and parked them on his knobby nose. With a dramatic flair he unfurled the letter and began to read . . .

Don't fool yourselves. Those who live immoral lives, who are idol worshipers, adulterers or homosexuals—will have no share in his kingdom. Neither will thieves or greedy people, drunkards, slanderers, or robbers.

He paused, peering at the audience over the top of his glasses. Then continued . . .

There was a time when some of you were just like that but now your sins are washed away, and you are set apart for God, and he has accepted you because of what the Lord Jesus Christ and the Spirit of our God have done for you (1 Corinthians 6:9-11 TLB).

"There was a time when some of you were just like that . . " —the words resonated in her soul.

She sighed. Before she met him, her life had been a blur of bed-hopping. How many beds? How many men? Each had whispered to her insecurity. Words never meant. Promises never kept. She had been an easy target—lonely and looking. But with every tryst her loneliness had only deepened.

One of three things, she had thought, would be her fate. Suicide. The psych ward. Or she would finally sink into a depravity which would turn her heart to stone.

A shudder and a smile simultaneously possessed her. A shudder as she recalled the most unpleasant experience of her life—and a smile as she thought about the most pleasant man she ever met.

As the sun's first rays had streaked the eastern sky, they had barged into her room. Pulling her from her bed, they hauled her into the street, as she tried to cover her nakedness with a skimpy gown grabbed from the foot of the bed.

They had stormed through the streets and crashed through the crowds, dragging her to her appointment with death.

Charging through the Temple doors, they had shoved her to the floor at the feet of the teacher.

"We caught her," they shrieked—"caught her in bed with her neighbor's husband! The law says to stone her. What do you say?"

Nothing. That's what he said. *Nothing.*

Instead, he stooped and began writing in the dirt with his finger. Annoyed by the snub, they pressed him: "What do you say?" they demanded.

Slowly he stood. Distinctly he spoke . . .

Let the one among you who has never sinned throw the first stone at her (John 8:7 JBP).

Again he stooped, and again he wrote in the dirt.

One after another they stooped, too, to lay their rocks on the ground. And one after another they edged to the door.

When he looked up, the crowd had dwindled to two—just him and her.

"Where are they?" he asked. "Has no one condemned you?"

"No, sir."

"Neither do I. Go now and leave your life of sin."

What had begun as the darkest day of her life became the brightest. "He gave me a new life," she mused. "He knew my sin, but he saw my life as an unfinished story, and he gave me a clean page on which to begin the next chapter."[1]

The minute heaven's gate swings open I intend to go looking for this lady, because she has the answer to a question that has gnawed at me for years: *What did Jesus write in the dirt?* Have you wondered about that, too?

He could have just been buying time by doodling, I suppose. But I don't think so. May I give you my guess? I think he was writing something that he wanted her accusers to see.

Maybe he was countering their question with one of his own: *Why is she alone? Why didn't you bring the man?*

Or maybe he was scribbling the sins of the censors, forcing them to face their own less-than-laudable lives—their lusts, their hypocrisy.

You've never done what she's done, but have you ever wanted to?

You haven't slept with your neighbor's wife, but have you lusted for her in your heart?

They had swaggered into the Temple spouting the law: *The law says to stone her!* From a purely legal standpoint they were, of course, correct. Jesus didn't deny that. But with fifteen words he qualified the critics.

> Let the one among you who has never sinned throw the first stone at her.

He forced them (and us) to look at law in the mirror of morals.

You want to kill her? You are judicially justified, but are you morally qualified? Your hands are clean, but is your heart? Are you fit to judge her? You want to stone her? Go ahead, stone her. But put your best man forward—the man who has never sinned. He is the one who should throw the first stone.

Does that make you as uncomfortable as it does me? You see, they had the goods on her. I've passed judgment with far less. Flimsy evidence. Suspect sources. Slashing speculation. Callused innuendo. In the wake of office (or church) gossip lie the bleached bones of wrecked reputations and ruined relationships.

> Woe to you, Pharisees, and you religious leaders! You are like beautiful mausoleums—full of dead men's bones, and of foulness and corruption. You try to look like saintly men, but underneath those pious robes of yours are hearts besmirched with every sort of hypocrisy and sin (Matthew 23:27-28 TLB).

Only one person in that Temple crowd was qualified to throw a stone. Only one had never sinned. And he—don't miss this—*he neither condoned nor condemned!* Most of us feel compelled to do one or the other. Jesus was perfectly comfortable doing neither.

He didn't condone her conduct. He called her sin what it

was—*sin*. And challenged her to change. He loved her too much to sanction her self-destructive behavior in the name of compassion.

But neither did he condemn her. He knew that she had made some sorry choices, taken some wrong turns. But he also knew that her life was an unfinished story. So he offered her another chance. A fresh start.

You've probably already discovered it, but in case you haven't, I must make a confession—I exercised considerable literary license at the beginning of this chapter. The truth is we don't know what this woman did after her encounter with Jesus.

"Go now and leave your life of sin," he urged.

Did she?

I don't know. But I know she could have. He never asks the impossible. She could change if she wanted to.

So can I.

So can you.

Your life, like hers, is an unfinished story. Whenever you're ready to write the next chapter, he has a fresh page for you.

CHAPTER 14

BOUGHT AND PAID FOR

*"So you're the little woman who wrote the
book that made this great war!"*

So spoke Abraham Lincoln when he was introduced to
Harriet Beecher Stowe in 1862.

The book was *Uncle Tom's Cabin*, Stowe's novel that
compelled the country to confront the shame of slavery.

May I refresh your memory?[1]

Mr. Shelby had speculated recklessly, and was deeply in
debt. Mr. Haley, a slave-trader who held most of Shelby's notes,
was salivating at the prospect of foreclosure. Shelby's only way
out was to barter some of his slaves for those notes.

Uncle Tom had been a Shelby slave since he was just a
child. Good-hearted, hard-working, loyal. The thought of selling
him was almost more than Shelby could bear. But the hard-
hearted Haley refused to drop the debt unless he got Tom.

So Uncle Tom said sad good-byes to his weeping wife, Chloe,
his two fine sons and his baby daughter, and rode away from his
old Kentucky home, sitting in shackles beside the slimy slave-trader.

Shelby's wife and their 13-year-old son, Master George,
were crushed. Uncle Tom was like a member of the family.
Mrs. Shelby solemnly swore that somehow, some way, some
day, she would buy Tom back.

Several years later Tom was put up for auction at a slave warehouse in New Orleans, where he was bought by the despicable Simon Legree.

Shortly after he bought him, Legree became livid when Tom refused his order to flog a female slave. Savagely kicking him in the head with his heavy boot, he howled, "An't I yer master? Didn't I pay down twelve hundred dollars, cash, for all there is inside yer old cussed black shell? An't yer mine, now, body and soul?"

"No!" said Tom, blood pooling in the corners of his mouth, "No! my soul an't yours, Mas'r! You haven't bought it, —ye can't buy it! It's been bought and paid for, by one that is able to keep it."

"How would ye like to be tied to a tree, and have a slow fire lit up around ye; —wouldn't that be pleasant, —eh, Tom?"

"Mas'r," said Tom, "I know ye can do dreadful things . . . but, after ye've killed the body, there an't no more ye can do. And O, there's all eternity to come, after that!"

ETERNITY—the word thrilled through the black man's soul with light and power, as he spoke; it thrilled through the sinner's soul, too, like the bite of a scorpion.

But later, when Tom refused to rat on two runaway slaves, Legree forgot about eternity. Ranting with rage, he roared, "Well, Tom . . . I've made up my mind to kill you."

Tom was strung up in the shed by Sambo and Quimbo, two slaves that Legree had trained to be as ferocious as his bulldogs. They brutally beat Tom until Legree was convinced that he was dying. Through it all, Uncle Tom prayed for his miserable master.

His wondrous words and pious prayers had struck upon the hearts of the imbruted blacks, who had been the instruments of cruelty upon him; and, the instant Legree withdrew, they took him down . . .

"O, Tom!" said Quimbo, "we's been awful wicked to ye!"

"I forgive ye, with all my heart!" Tom said softly.

"O, Tom! do tell us who is Jesus, anyhow?" said Sambo; — "Jesus, that's been a standin' by you so, all this night!—Who is he?"

Battling for breath, Tom told them about Jesus—his life, his death, his everlasting presence, his power to save.

And they wept.

After the death of her husband, Mrs. Shelby started selling property. She had promised to buy Uncle Tom back, and she was set on making good on that promise.

Master George, now a strapping young man, started the search for Tom—a search that led at last to the plantation of the loathsome Legree.

He found him in the shed, where he had been lying two days in a stupor from the savage thrashing. Bending over his old friend he pleaded:

O, dear Uncle Tom! do wake—do speak once more! Look up! Here's Mas'r George—your own little Mas'r George. Don't you know me?

"Mas'r George!" said Tom feebly. "Mas'r George!" He looked bewildered.

Slowly the idea seemed to fill his soul; and the vacant eyes became fixed and brightened, the whole face lighted up, the hard hands clasped, and tears ran down the cheeks.

"Bless the Lord! it is—it is—it's all I wanted! They haven't forgot me. It warms my soul; it does my old heart good! Now I shall die content! Bless the Lord, oh my soul!"

"You shan't die! you mustn't die, nor think of it! I've come to buy you, and take you home . . ."

"O, Mas'r George, ye're too late. The Lord's bought me, and is going to take me home—and I long to go. Heaven is better than Kintuck."

He began to draw his breath with long, deep inspiration; and his broad chest rose and fell, heavily. The expression of his face was that of a conqueror.

"Who—who—who shall separate us from the love of Christ?" he said. And with a smile he fell asleep.

Sambo and Quimbo went with Master George to bury Uncle Tom. When they were done, George put a quarter in the hand of each and dismissed them.

But they lingered.

"If young Mas'r would please buy us," pleaded Sambo.

"We'd serve him so faithful!" promised Quimbo.

"Hard times here, Mas'r!" said Sambo. "Do, Mas'r, buy us, please!"

"I can't!—I can't!" Master George said emotionally. "It's impossible!"

Sambo and Quimbo hung their heads and slogged away in silence.

"O Tom! do tell us who is Jesus, anyhow? . . . Who is he?"

You can't hear about Jesus without wanting to know about him. You can't look at the life of Uncle Tom—or the apostle Paul or Albert Schweitzer or Mother Teresa—without wondering who he is, this one who inspires such a lay-down-your-life commitment.

Who is he?

He is . . .

 God.

 Man.

He is . . .

 A Prince.

 A King.

 A carpenter.

 A preacher.

 A friend.

He is . . .

Our High Priest.

Our Savior.

Our Redeemer.

Our mediator.

Our hope.

He is . . .

The sacrificial lamb.

The crucified Christ.

The resurrected Lord.

He is all of this and more.

He is the one—often the only one—who understands. He knows your concerns, your struggles, your heartaches. Even when you can't put them into words, he hears your heart.

"Hard times here, Master!"

"I know," he replies.

"Lord, I have problems—financial problems, family problems."

"I know."

"I am struggling with sadness, sickness, death."

"I know."

"I am discouraged, worried, depressed. Frustrated, disappointed, weak. Angry, hurt, lonely. Empty, broken, scared."

"I know."

"I haven't made the best use of my life."

"I know."

"I have sinned."

"I know."

"Master, buy me, please!"

"Done! That's why I came. To rescue you from slavery. To pay your ransom. To redeem you. To set you free."[2]

O victory in Jesus,
My Savior, forever,
He sought me and bo't me
with His redeeming blood.[3]

CHAPTER 15

HIS GRACE IS
SUFFICIENT FOR YOU

He stormed through the front door, screaming like a burglar alarm. My son, Doug. When he was four years old.

What had happened?

Had Ike (that was his dog) been run over by a truck?

Had he wandered into the weeds in the alley (he had a habit of that) and been bitten by a rattlesnake?

Had a feisty friend (he had a few) smacked him with a two-by-four?

No, none of the above. *He had a splinter in his finger!*

His mother went to the medicine cabinet for tweezers and alcohol. (That's when the needle pegged out on the scream meter.) She carefully removed the splinter, bathed the tiny puncture in alcohol, and examined it from every angle. Serious as a surgeon.

I was amused. "Why such a fuss over a *little* splinter?" I asked.

Mistake! Big mistake!

She gave me a look that would wilt an artificial flower. "That *little* splinter," she snapped, "could cause an infection . . . which could invade his body . . . which could kill him! I repeat, *which . . . could . . . kill . . . him!*"

No more questions.

Sin is like that splinter. It can cause lots of problems. It can attack your nervous system, affect your heartbeat, upset your digestion, and produce ulcers. It can wreck your mind and ruin your life. And it carries the germ of spiritual death.

If you step on a rusty nail, don't ignore it. Unless you clean the wound, you're inviting trouble.

Likewise, ignore sin at your own risk.

If it wasn't so serious, the way we deal with sin would be comical. I mean, we're like little children. Children scream, run, hide—do anything to escape the sting of sterilizing a wound.

Run *to* God, not *from* God, with your sin. Let him cleanse your wound and eliminate your pain.

A couple of things need to be said here.

First, God loves you whatever your sin!

I didn't stop loving my son because he speared his finger with a splinter. Know what? I would love him if he had done something far more foolish and harmful. In fact, I can't think of anything he could do—anything at all—that would keep me from loving him. That's the way fathers are.

God loves you no matter what you have done. That's the way fathers are.

Second, forgive yourself whatever your sin!

Can you imagine my son spending the rest of his life hammering himself for having stabbed his finger with a splinter? I can't either.

Don't spend another day, another minute, beating up on yourself for having made a mistake, no matter what it is. Turn to God for treatment and get on with your life.

Do you have time for a couple of stories that are fresh in my memory?

A man who was teetering near the edge of emotional collapse came to see me a few days ago. He had problems, big problems. His world was falling apart. His business was in shambles, and his marriage wasn't far behind.

The reason for his anguish was a mistake he had made years ago. The memory of it nagged him constantly, plagued him unmercifully. He was so consumed with guilt that he couldn't function.

He was a good-hearted man, sincerely sorry for his sin. He had confessed it. And tried to forget it. Unsuccessfully.

We read and discussed an appropriate scripture. (I'm going to share it with you in a minute.) And we prayed. He was feeling better when he left. But a week later he was back, in the same self-condemning condition.

"God must be sad," I said.

"Why?" he asked.

"Because you don't trust him."

"Yes I do."

"No you don't."

"Why do you say that?"

"Because he promised to forgive you, and you don't trust him to do it."

Do you? Do you trust him? Accept his forgiveness?

Second story.

I spent a half-hour recently with a lady who wouldn't let me talk. She hogged the conversation, slamming herself non-stop for a sin she had committed as a teenager.

Finally she paused, and asked, "Will you pray for me and ask God to forgive me?"

"I'm sorry," I said, "but I can't do that. God wouldn't even know what we were talking about."

"What?"

"Isn't this the same thing we prayed about the last time you came to see me?" I asked.

"Well . . . yes."

"Didn't we ask God to forgive you?"

"Yes."

"The Bible promises that when God forgave you, he forgot your sin," I said. "Wouldn't it be an insult to him to question his promise?"

Does God really make that promise? That he will forget our sins? He sure does. *"I will forgive and forget their sins,"* he says (Jeremiah 31:34 TLB). When he forgives, he forgets!

I'm not a doctor, but I occasionally give prescriptions. For people suffering with agonizing guilt, I prescribe strong doses of Psalm 51. (This is the scripture I read with the man I mentioned a few paragraphs back.)

Psalm 51 is King David's prayer of confession, and plea for forgiveness. Why don't you get your Bible and read this chapter? Right now. Go ahead. Then we'll talk about it.

Finished?

Okay, let's look at a few sentences in David's prayer.

"Have mercy on me, O God" (verse 1).

I overheard a conversation in a pizza parlor yesterday. Actually, it wasn't a conversation, it was a monologue. "I don't do church!" said the woman who was holding court. "But I'm basically a good person, and . . ."

I didn't listen to the rest of her lecture. Didn't need to. I knew where she was going with it . . . *Justice would demand that God reward her goodness.*

David had a different take on it. *Justice?* Forget it! He didn't want justice, he wanted *mercy!* He made no attempt to offset his vices with his virtues. He could have, you know. He had done a lot of good. He was a good king. His job-rating scored high in the polls.

Besides, God himself had chosen him to be king. Chosen him because of his good heart.

David's name appears in the Bible more than any other—over 1,000 times. And he was called a man after God's own heart. Stout credentials, don't you agree?

But David didn't work the phones and blitz the talk-shows with a cadre of PR people in a campaign of damage-control. He didn't offer a single argument in his defense. Didn't try to bargain with God. Didn't attempt to put a favorable face on his sin.

He threw himself on God's mercy. That was his only hope. *"Have mercy on me, O God!"* he pleaded.

"Glad to!" God responded.

Mercy! It's our only hope too. And something God is glad to give. He delights in showing mercy (Micah 7:18).

"I know my transgressions, and my sin is always before me" (verse 3).

Moy Ling was a superb craftsman, a carver of fine stones. Learned the art from his father.

Moy was sculpting a bracelet from a beautiful, very expensive, piece of jade. Just as he was finishing, his carving tool slipped and made a tiny nick in one of the flowers.

When Moy's father saw the completed bracelet, he was thrilled with his son's exquisite work. It would bring a good price. "No, father," said Moy, "the bracelet is flawed." He pointed out the imperfection, which even the expert eye of his father had not detected.

"I know my transgressions," said David. His sins—hidden from others—were hideously conspicuous to him. I know the feeling, don't you?

"My sin is always before me," he said.

He never walked on his balcony without remembering an earlier walk there when he watched Bathsheba bathe.

He never put his head on his pillow without remembering going to bed with someone who didn't belong to him.

He never reached for his pen or sent a servant on an errand without remembering issuing the warrant that sealed a faithful soldier's death.

Knowledge of his sin was a constant companion, always pointing its crooked, accusing finger at him.

Guilty? Yes! Weary of living with guilt? Double yes!

"Sprinkle me with the cleansing blood and I shall be clean again. Wash me and I shall be whiter than snow" (verse 7).

Refreshing thought. It had been a long time since David had felt clean. And he wanted to feel it again. Wanted to be washed, cleansed, purified.

"Create in me a pure heart, O God" (verse 10).

David wasn't asking for forgiveness here. He already had that. When the prophet Nathan confronted him with his sin, David didn't dodge. He simply said, "I have sinned against the Lord." And Nathan's immediate response was, "The Lord has taken away your sin" (2 Samuel 12:13). That's how fast God forgives.

I hope you didn't miss that point. Let me say it another way. The turnaround time between confession of sin and forgiveness of sin is zero! When you approach God with guilt in your heart and confession on your lips, forgiveness is yours before you put the period at the end of the sentence.

David knew he had been forgiven. But he wanted more. Not just pardon, but purity. Not just a new start, but a new nature. Not just angioplasty, but a new heart. A heart transplant, that's what David wanted. He wanted his diseased heart replaced with a new one—*"filled with clean thoughts and right desires."*

"Restore to me the joy of your salvation" (verse 12).

David had once known the joy of salvation. But he had made a lousy trade, exchanging a God-centered life for a self-centered, sin-centered one. And he had learned that sin and joy can't live together, that they are incompatible roommates.

He had a desperate sense of loss. He hadn't lost salvation, but he had lost the joy of it. He lived in luxury, had everything the world could give. But he had lost the joy of salvation, lost what the world cannot give. And he wanted it back.

Adultery! Murder! Those were the most obvious sins of David. I mention this just in case you're wondering if your sins are too vile to be forgiven.

Listen to me! The door David entered to be with God is wide enough for all. It's no accident that God turned a couple of the worst sinners into a couple of the best saints—David in the Old Testament and Paul in the New Testament. Here's how Paul said it:

> Christ Jesus came into the world to save sinners—of whom I am the worst. But for that very reason I was shown mercy so that in me, the worst of sinners, Christ Jesus might display his unlimited patience as an example for those who would believe on him and receive eternal life (1 Timothy 1:15-16).

Don't even think about putting a limit on God's mercy. The blood of Jesus cleanses from *all sin* (1 John 1:7). Whatever your sin, the bandage is wider than the wound.

Looking at the past, we see much to humble us. Looking to God, we see everything to encourage us.

In Psalm 51 David came clean. He told God everything and asked for forgiveness.

What was the result? I'll let him tell you . . .

> There was a time when I wouldn't admit what a sinner I was. But my dishonesty made me miserable and filled my days with frustration. All day and all night your hand was heavy on me. My

strength evaporated like water on a sunny day until I finally admitted all my sins to you and stopped trying to hide them. I said to myself, "I will confess them to the Lord." And you forgave me! All my guilt is gone (Psalm 32:3-5 TLB).

I think Psalm 51 is a pretty good prescription, don't you?

John Bunyan compared his spiritual journey to a pair of balance scales. The right-hand weighing pan was his *despair* and the left-hand pan was his *hope.*

His pilgrimage consisted of three phases. First, the right-hand pan (despair) was full and the left-hand pan (hope) was empty. Second, for awhile they were evenly balanced. And third, the left-hand pan (hope) was full and the right-hand pan (despair) was empty.

In the first phase, Bunyan was tormented with guilt. Despair was heavy. Hope was weightless. There was, he felt, no hope for him.

In the second phase, a piece of a sentence of scripture nudged its way into his mind—*My grace is sufficient!* Maybe there was hope after all. Yet, he couldn't bring himself to believe that grace included him. Others perhaps, but not him.

Eventually he discovered the problem. He had put only four of the six words that make up the sentence in the pan that held *hope.* He had placed *My grace is sufficient* on the scale—but the full sentence says *My grace is sufficient for thee!* "Because the *for thee* was left out, I was not contented," he wrote.

But in the third phase—the victorious phase—the *for thee* found its place in his heart. Despair vanished and the "sufficiency of grace prevailed with peace and joy." *Hope* now held all the weight. *Despair* held none.

Listen carefully! It is always easier to believe that there is grace *for the world* than it is to believe that there is grace *for you.*

Martin Luther believed completely and preached confidently that Jesus died for the world long before he was convinced that Jesus died for *Martin Luther.*

As a young man, John Wesley crossed the Atlantic to preach forgiveness to the Indians. But not until he reached middle-age did he accept the possibility of forgiveness for *John Wesley.*

Forgiveness isn't just *for the world,* my friend. It is *for you!*

> *What happiness for those whose guilt has been forgiven! What joys when sins are covered over! What relief for those who have confessed their sins and God has cleared their record (Psalm 32:1-2 TLB).*

Do you see the gifts in that text?

Happiness!

Joy!

Relief!

You can have these gifts of grace. And they won't cost you a dime. They are covered by insurance, and the premium has already been paid. It is God's gift to you (Ephesians 2:8).

His grace is sufficient *FOR YOU!*

CHAPTER 16

THAT'S WHERE
YOU BELONG

She was a very pretty girl. Soft blond hair. Striking green eyes. Delicate features. She looked wholesome and innocent. Like a typical high school kid. A cheerleader, or a member of the choir. She said she was seventeen. She looked even younger to me.

She spoke in a soft, quiet voice. Her vocabulary and grammar were impressive, blending into crisp, intelligent sentences.

"He told me he loved me," she said. "And he said if I loved him, I would work for him. I worked a truck stop. Four girls have disappeared from there. The police think they're dead. I was terrified. They'd drive me forty or fifty miles out on the Interstate, and then turn down a dark road. It's scary out there."

Her voice trembled. "I was beaten by one of the truckers. He was on something. Pot or coke. Crack maybe."

She stopped talking, lost in tormenting images that were bursting behind her eyes. She brushed a tear from her cheek.

"I am so ashamed," she said slowly. "I . . . I know he didn't love me." She tried to say it matter-of-factly, but her eyes brimmed with tears.

"You're going home tonight? To Colorado?" I asked.

"Yes. I called my mother. She and Dad want me to come home. They miss me. My brother and sisters do, too."

"Did you tell her what you've been doing the past three months, since you ran away?"

She nodded.

"They love me. I'm excited about going home, but it's going to be hard."

She smiled for the first time. She was really a very pretty little girl.

"I'm glad they want you back."

"Me, too," she said. "I miss them. I am so happy I'm going home."

So was I. I'm glad she woke up before it was too late. Glad she didn't numb her pain and pickle her brain with drugs. Glad she didn't give up on herself. Glad she remembered home.

Home. That's where she belonged.

It's reminiscent of a very old story—the story of a boy who selfishly sliced a piece out of his father's heart.[1]

"I want my share of the estate now, instead of waiting until you die!" he squawked.

A few days later he packed his bag, pocketed his cash, and headed for the big city. He cut a sorry figure there, wasting his money on parties and prostitutes until his pockets were empty.

He had never experienced hunger before, but he did now. And that forced him into another new experience—he had to look for a job. Since this pampered prodigal had never had to work, he was qualified for only one available job . . . feeding pigs.

From spoiled son, to swinging single, to slop slinger.

It made him think. He had plenty of time for that. There was nothing to interrupt his thoughts except the occasional grunt of a pig, his gnawing hunger, and a stinging conscience.

So he thought. And he came to his senses. That's the hinge on which this part of the story swings—*he came to his senses.*

"I will go back to my father," he said.

154

Not without misgivings I'm sure. He had, after all, fractured his father's heart and squandered half the estate his dad had grown old and tired acquiring.

Even so, he could never have imagined how much his father missed him. He tiptoed into his son's vacant room every night and reminisced. He ran his callused fingers over the beat-up Little League cap, and remembered the bright eyes and freckled nose of his boy beneath it. Many a night he held the framed photograph of his son in his gnarled hands and examined every angle and contour of his handsome face. And smiled. And wept.

My, how he missed him.

The boy missed his dad, too. He hadn't expected that. Dad, who was light-years behind the times. Dad, who worked hard instead of smart. Dad, who sometimes didn't seem to have both oars in the water.

Dad . . .

Home . . .

He thought of his junk-filled room. His rumpled bed. The towel on the doorknob. The photos on the wall of . . . of so many good times.

He thought of the family banter—clichés and silly jokes that had meaning only to them. And of Dad's cap on the nail in the hall, the silent sign that he was home. And of the playful punch . . . wink . . . nod.

But what triggered the sudden gush of tears was the memory of the end-of-evening ritual. He'd never really thought about it before. It was invariably the same—exactly at the stroke of ten dad would stand, stretch, and say, "Goodnight, all."

"Goodnight, honey."

"G'night, dad."

He ached for that exchange tonight. Tears washed his leathery, sunburned face. Finger-combing his mud-matted hair he stood up straight and tall . . .

"I'm going home!" he said.

And he did.

I can almost hear the voices in the midnight darkness. Listen.

"G'night, dad."

"Goodnight, son."

"Dad?"

"Yes."

"I'm glad I'm home."

"Me, too, son. Me, too."

Home. That's where he belonged.

That's where you belong, too.

Thomas Wolfe said, "You can't go home again." He was wrong. God's story of the straying son says, *"You can go home again!"*

If you are away, he misses you more than you can imagine. He wants you to come home. Will you? That's where you belong.

I can almost hear your voices . . .

"Father?"

"Yes."

"I'm glad I'm home."

"Me, too, child! Me, too!"

CHAPTER 17

LET'S BE FRIENDS

She was standing in the corner of the church foyer. Alone. Dozens of people were nearby, huddled in cliquish knots. Chatting. Laughing.

But she was alone.

I would soon learn that she was a newly-enrolled university student. And that she came from a rural community with less population than the school she was attending. Even less than the church she was visiting.

I walked over to speak to her. Before I finished "Hello" she exploded in tears.

"Can I help?" I asked.

"I'm so homesick," she said. "I don't have any friends here. I don't know anyone and I feel so alone."

Alone. Friendless. My, that hurts.

Few things produce deeper pain than being friendless. And few things, greater joy than a faithful friend.

I saw them in a neighbor's yard as I jogged by—a little freckled-faced beauty, whispering a don't-tell-a-soul secret to her playmate. They covered their mouths with pudgy palms, and giggled. Then, holding hands, skipped off to play.

Friends!

It's something you never outgrow, this need for bosom-buddy friendship. You quit whispering and giggling. Maybe. But you continue to crave camaraderie with that one-in-a-million person, that intimate friend.

Shared experiences are special. Unshared ones sterile. An unshared sunset loses some of its beauty. An unshared book loses some of its pleasure. An unshared anything loses some of its joy.

Whether experiencing the sweet taste of success or the bitter flavor of failure, you want to share it with someone. Someone special. Someone close. Someone who cares. A friend.

Some wit defined friendship as the relationship a woman has with a man when she'd rather knot. (Sorry. I've had an itch to use that line for a long time.)

Levity aside, how can we define friendship?

It's not easy. Let me give it a try by telling you about my best friend, because he is the most eloquent definition of friendship I know. When I think of him, I feel warm all over and secure deep down. Why? Because I know I can talk to him about anything . . .

My successes.

My failures.

My hopes.

My struggles.

My weaknesses.

My fears.

My deepest feelings.

Anything!

And I know how he will respond. He will be gratified by my victories and grieved by my defeats. He shares my song and my sorrow, my life and my load. And he accepts me as I am. Unconditionally.

No birth certificate is issued when a friendship is born. But at that moment life takes on new meaning. It is enlarged and enriched. Pleasure is expanded. Pain is diminished.

An old definition of friendship by George Eliot runs this way:

> *A friend is one to whom we may pour out the contents of our hearts, chaff and grain together, knowing that the gentlest of hands will sift it, keep what is worth keeping, and with a breath of kindness blow the rest away.*

Do you know that God wants to be your friend? Seems strange in a way. It is uncommon for people on different social, educational, or economic levels to become close friends. Presidents don't generally pal with peasants. University professors don't normally fraternize with grade-school dropouts. Six-figure executives don't ordinarily socialize with street people. We usually form friendship with those who are like us.

If the bank president and the apprentice clerk, because of their differences, seldom become close friends, it seems unlikely that the God who owns the world and keeps the universe ticking would want to hang out with a gal who can't balance her checkbook or a guy who can't fix a leaky faucet. If well-heeled residents of Beverly Hills shun down-and-out tenants of Watts, it seems doubtful that a glorious God would want to mingle with shabby sinners.

Doubts notwithstanding, God wants to be your friend.

He knew that would be a stretch for us. Knew we would find it hard to feel close to someone so superior—and so far away. So he took an astounding step to bridge the gap. Since we couldn't become like him and go where he is, he became like us and came where we are. He stepped down from his throne, took off his robe, changed into his work clothes, and moved into our neighborhood.

> *. . . he gave up all he had, and took the nature of a servant. He became like man and appeared in human likeness (Philippians 2:7 TEV).*

He wanted us to know that he knows how we feel. So he went through everything we experience—birth, infancy, childhood, adolescence, adulthood. Just like us.

He got hungry, thirsty, tired, sick, lonely. Just like us.

He walked in our shoes and went nose-to-nose with the same temptations that tangle with us.

> *Our High Priest is not one who cannot feel sympathy for our weaknesses. On the contrary, we have a High Priest who was tempted in every way that we are . . . (Hebrews 4:15 TEV).*

Everyone felt the sincerity and warmth of his friendship. Tiny tots and senile seniors. Winners and losers. Top guns and wayward sons. Crooks and cripples. Prostitutes and puritans. Drop-outs and do-gooders.

He was called a friend of sinners (Matthew 11:19). And he was that. He was, in fact, the ultimate friend. *"The greatest love,"* he said, *"is shown when a person lays down his life for his friends"* (John 15:13 TLB).

And then he did just that—laid down his life for us, his friends.

> *He humbled himself and became obedient to death—even death on a cross! (Philippians 2:8).*

The cross! The final blow. The end. When the last nail was set, his enemies thought they'd done him in. It sure seemed that way.

But they were wrong! This was his doing, not theirs. He *chose* to live—and die—for his friends. For me. For you.

It was his way of saying, "Let's be friends. Best friends."

CHAPTER 18

ONLY ONE THING MATTERS

He could see them clearly from the cockpit of his Grumman Wildcat F4F—nine twin-engine Japanese bombers on course to their target, the aircraft carrier *Lexington*.

He was flying alone. Unless he attacked, the *Lexington* and her crew were done for. Hands sweating, he squeezed the controls. The engine roared and the Wildcat lunged. He dumped five of the nine bombers in the Pacific, chased the other four into retreat, and saved the *Lexington*.

Lieutenant Commander Edward Henry "Butch" O'Hare, the Navy's number one World War II ace, became the first naval aviator to receive the Congressional Medal of Honor. He didn't survive the war. Died in combat a year later. But Chicago, his hometown, wouldn't let the memory of his bravery die. If you ever fly into Chicago's *O'Hare International Airport*, you'll know for whom it was named, and why.

But that's not the whole story. For that, we have to back up a couple of decades, to the Chicago of the Roaring Twenties. And a name you'll recognize—Al Capone.

One of Capone's cronies in crime was nicknamed "Artful Eddie." Eddie was a lawyer. A brilliant one. The most ruthless rogues of the mob beat the rap due to the skill of "Artful Eddie."

Al Capone handpicked Eddie to run the dog tracks nation-wide. He became the undisputed czar of illegal dog racing. Overnight he became outrageously rich.

Then one day, for no apparent reason, Eddie turned himself in. He wanted to go straight he said, and was ready to sing.

The cops were skeptical. Not just because Eddie was offer-ing to give up his gold-plated gambling empire, but because of what it meant to rat on the mob. Didn't Eddie know?

He knew.

So what was the catch?

Simple. Eddie explained that he'd spent his life in the gutter of crime. But he'd been thinking. After all was said and done, there was only one thing that really mattered to him. His son.

His son deserved a chance. Deserved a decent name and the memory of his dad doing the right thing. So Eddie sang.

And the mob retaliated. Two shotgun blasts ended Eddie.

And his son? He was accepted at Annapolis. Became a Navy flying ace. Dumped five Japanese bombers in the Pacific, and received the Congressional Medal of Honor. Lieutenant Commander Edward Henry "Butch" O'Hare.

So if you ever fly into Chicago's *O'Hare International Airport*, give a silent salute to a hero, Butch O'Hare. And to his daddy, Edward J. "Artful Eddie" O'Hare, the crook who decided to go straight so his boy would have a chance. And paid for it with his life.[1]

Different time. Different place. Different story.

Some claimed he was genius; others said he was insane. He was a hero to some, a brassy braggart to others.

He was a splinter under the fingernail, that's for sure. For one thing, he was forever defending the underdog. He got in the face of hotshot religious leaders who preened and strutted and condemned. He popped their balloons of judgmental arrogance and stood his ground until they slithered away humiliated.

When they attempted to publicly discredit him, his responses were devastating. He detonated their loaded questions with such simple answers that they looked like fools for asking them.

His offenses were irritating and intimidating, but never violent. Certainly not criminal. Yet he became Number 1 on the *Most Wanted* list. The religious-political establishment was set on nailing him. Their aim was clear—they wanted him eliminated!

Constant surveillance and harassment dogged him for three years. There was no way out. He knew that. So one day he told his confidants that he was going to turn himself in.

What?!! Was he crazy? His enemies weren't distributing *Wanted: Dead or Alive!* posters. They wanted him *dead!* Period!

Turn himself in? Didn't he know what that would mean?

He knew.

He leaked the time and place where he could be found, and a mob of soldiers showed up, armed to the teeth. What were they afraid of? An ambush? Afraid that he might decide to go out in a blaze of glory?

He taunted them. He didn't resist arrest, he invited it.

They wasted no time. They arrested him, started the trial the same night, and had their verdict by morning.

Some trial. It was raw travesty. The prosecution's case was fabricated, backed by hired witnesses who lied and bungled their lines.

The only witness for the defense came as a surprise—the judge himself. He found no basis for the charges, he said. Three times he moved to release him. And three times he stared into

167

the angry eyes of mutiny. Finally he caved in.

Court adjourned. They got their death sentence. And carried it out the same day.

No merciful end-it-quickly shotgun blast here. No, this was a slow, brutal, excruciating execution. A cross. Sweat. Spit. Flies. Pain. Blood.

"Artful Eddie" did an admirable thing, but an understandable one.

Jesus did an admirable thing, but one that defies human understanding.

He didn't deserve to die. A thief who died beside him said it best: *"We deserve to die for our evil deeds, but this man hasn't done one thing wrong"* (Luke 23:4 TLB).

He didn't have to die. He could have called angels to rescue him (Matthew 26:53).

He didn't *deserve* to die. He didn't *have* to die. He *chose* to die.

Why?

Simple. After all is said and done, there is only one thing that really matters to him. You!

He wanted you to have a chance.

CHAPTER 19

IT IS FINISHED

Tetelestai.

Ever heard that word? It's a Greek word. One you need to know.

Now don't get the fidgets. I'm not going to have you conjugating Greek verbs. (I couldn't grade your paper anyhow.) But this word is important, and you need to be acquainted with it. So stay with me, and at the end of the story I'm about to relate, I'll tell you what it means.

Ebenezer Wooton (really, that was his name), was an evangelist in England in the nineteenth century. He had just completed a series of summer evening services. The benediction had been intoned, the flock had scattered, and the parson was packing.

A young man came out of the shadows, approached the preacher and asked, "Mr. Wooton, what must I do to be saved?"

Without looking up Wooton replied, "Too late! Too late, my friend, too late!"

"Oh, don't say that!" the youth pleaded.

"Yes, my friend," he said, now looking into his eyes, "it's too late! You want to know what *you must do* to be saved, and I tell you that you are hundreds of years too late! The work of

171

salvation is done, completed, finished! It was finished on the cross. Jesus said so with the last breath that he drew!"

He was referring, of course, to John's account of Jesus' final words:

Jesus said, "It is finished." With that, he bowed his head and gave up his spirit (John 19:30).

And this is where we are introduced to the word *tetelestai—it is finished*. It meant that a work was completed, finished to perfection.

When an artist brushed the final stroke on his canvas, stepped back and examined his creation and found nothing that could be improved, he would say with satisfaction, *Tetelestai!*

Through the twisting trails of his three-year ministry, Jesus was really walking in a straight line—straight to the cross. The cross was the final stroke on the canvas.

He didn't step back and *view* the picture; he *was* the picture. He didn't stand on the sideline and *watch* the finish; he *was* the finish. When he drew his last labored breath, his work was finished, completed to perfection. So with that final breath he said, *Tetelestai—It is finished*.

This morning, as I was working on this chapter, a longtime friend, Carrie Hamilton, stopped by for a visit. It was a welcomed and refreshing recess, bringing back a lot of warm memories.

W. T. Hamilton, Carrie's late husband, was my wife's minister in Lamesa, Texas, when we married. I was an aspiring young preacher, just out of college, greener than grass. W. T. took me under his wing, becoming a teacher and mentor, and one of my dearest friends. He treated me as an equal. I wasn't. Nowhere close. Never will be. But that's how he treated me.

I miss him. He's been gone twelve years. In the waning hours of his life, sensing the approach of death, he said to his brother-in-law, "It's happening too fast. I wanted to get Carrie moved before I left." He was a meticulous man, and his affairs were in excellent order. Still, he wished for a little more time for the finishing touch, the final stroke on the canvas.

Henry Buckle would have understood. Buckle was writing his book, *History of Civilization*, when he was downed by a disabling fever. In his delirium he babbled about his book. "Oh, to finish my book!" And with the words "My book! My book!" he died.

Venerable Bede would have understood too. Bede—more than twelve centuries ago—tackled the task of translating the Gospel of John into English. As the translation neared completion, death threatened. The elderly scholar was racked with pain. He couldn't sleep. He could barely breathe. Could he possibly live until his translation was finished?

He hired a young man to read to him from the original text. He would then dictate to him the English equivalent. Day and night they pushed on to complete the work.

At last they came to the final sentence of the final chapter. "Master, only one sentence remains!" said the secretary. He read the words and Bede feebly translated them.

"It is finished, master!" said the young scribe.

"Aye, it is finished! Lift me up, place me at that window of my cell at which I have so often prayed to God. Now glory be to the Father and to the Son and to the Holy Ghost!" And with those words he died.

I am identifying with these feelings tonight, as I write the next-to-last chapter of this book. I'm grateful that by God's grace I am being permitted to complete it. When I draft the last sentence, I will take a deep breath, thank God for his goodness and guidance—and for you, the reader—and stare into space for awhile. I will be glad that it is finished.

But the finished work of Christ—ah—that is the finish that saved our souls and set the angels singing.

Jesus wasn't afraid that he would die before he finished his work. He *had* to die to finish it. Finishing and dying were one and the same. If you can get a grip on that, it will change you forever.

Just ask James Hudson Taylor.

Taylor is best known for his missionary work in China. But China would never have heard of Hudson Taylor had it not been for what he described in his old age as "a day that he could never forget."

It was a day from his youth. A holiday. Everyone was gone from home and Hudson was bored. He sauntered into his father's library and searched the shelves for something that interested him. Nothing did. But rummaging through an old basket, he found a pamphlet that captured his attention—*The Finished Work of Christ.*

He scampered off to the stable loft, sunk in the hay, and started reading. He was mesmerized by the message—*The Finished Work of Christ.* "If," he asked himself, "if the whole work was finished, and the whole debt paid upon the cross, what is there left for me to do? And then," he said, "there dawned on me the joyous conviction that there was nothing in the world to be done but to fall upon my knees, accept the Saviour, and praise him for evermore." He slipped out of the soft hay, knelt on the hard floor, and surrendered to the Savior.

The whole work was finished and the whole debt paid on the cross. In his death he finished what he came to do—he redeemed us.

> . . . It was not with perishable things such as silver or gold that you were redeemed . . . but with the precious blood of Christ, a lamb without blemish or defect (1 Peter 1:18-19).

He paid the price. And what a price! He assumed our sins, accepted our sentence, and took our place.

Do you recall Charles Dickens' touching story about the heroic Sydney Carton?[1]

Sydney Carton felt that he had done nothing of worth in his life. Now he saw his chance to change that. You see, he looked enough like Charles Darnay to be his twin. Carton had no family. Charles Darnay had a wife and child—and he was in prison, sentenced to die.

Sydney Carton had a plan. But there wasn't much time, for the execution was scheduled to be carried out within the hour. He went to Darnay's cell and convinced him to exchange clothes with him. Darnay walked out free, and Carton took his place in prison.

Within minutes he was ushered into a dimly-lighted room with fifty-one other prisoners who were to be beheaded that day. The death-carts that would carry them to the guillotine could be heard rumbling through the gate.

A frail seamstress, mistaking Carton for Darnay, came across the room to speak to him. "Will you let me hold your hand?" she asked. "It will give me courage."

As she looked at him, he saw doubt, and then astonishment in her eyes. He pressed her work-worn fingers and touched his lips, pleading with her to be silent.

"Are you dying for him?" she whispered.

"And his wife and child. Hush! Yes."

"Oh, will you let me hold your brave hand, stranger?"

"Hush! Yes, my poor sister, to the last."

As Sydney Carton ascended the scaffold to die for Charles Darnay and his wife and child, he contemplated the result of his sacrifice:

I see the lives for which I lay down my life, peaceful, useful, prosperous and happy, in that England which I shall see no more . . .

I see that I hold a sanctuary in their hearts and in the hearts of their descendants, generations hence. I see her, an old woman, weeping for me on the anniversary of this day . . .

He envisioned that they would have another baby, a boy, and that they would name the child for him. And he pictured this boy, when he had become a man, bringing his own son to this place, the very spot of his execution.

> . . . and I hear him tell the child my story, with a tender and a faltering voice.

The victory Jesus came to claim—our redemption—was finished at the cross. The work was complete. The finish was flawless.

That is why he triumphantly said, *Tetelestai!—It is finished!*

Come to the cross, dear reader, the very spot of his execution. And with tender and faltering voice say, *"Tetelestai!—It is finished; he took my place."*

CHAPTER 20

IT'S YOUR CHOICE

In this book I have tried to cement in your mind the certainty of your salvation, to convince you to trust the glorious promise that *"there is now no condemnation for those who are in Christ Jesus"* (Romans 8:1).
As Paul put it . . .

> . . . all of us who have been baptized into Christ Jesus were baptized into his death . . . We know that our old self was crucified with him . . . whoever has died is freed from sin (Romans 6:3, 6-7 NRSV).

I have written these chapters under the assumption that you have read his instructions, followed his directions, and *are in Christ Jesus, freed from sin.*

That may assume too much.

Revisiting Ebenezer Wooton

Was Ebenezer Wooton, the evangelist we met in the last chapter, right when he told that lad emerging from the shadows that there was nothing he could do, that "the work of salvation is done, completed, finished!"?

He was right that the work Jesus came to do—paying the price for our sins—is finished.

Did he mean there was *nothing* that young man needed to do? I don't think so either. He believed he needed to do *something* or he wouldn't have been conducting those evening preaching services.

You can hardly turn a page in your Bible without seeing statements that call for response . . .

Those who believe in the Son have eternal life, but those who do not obey the Son will never have life (John 3:36 NCV).

Repent and be baptized, every one of you . . . so that your sins may be forgiven (Acts 2:38).

He became the source of eternal salvation for all who obey him (Hebrews 5:9).

He does not want anyone to be destroyed but wants all to turn away from their sins (2 Peter 3:9 TEV).

Such statements cannot be ignored by a sincere seeker.

I know of no one (except a Universalist) who believes there is *nothing* you must do to be saved.

Let me give you an example. A friend recently sent me an audio cassette of a sermon his preacher had delivered the previous Sunday. Across the label was scrawled the word "Grace." Since that is my favorite subject, I eagerly shoved the tape into the cassette player in my car.

Making his best case for grace, the preacher said: "You are saved by grace, and only by grace. There isn't *anything* you need to do. There isn't *anything* you can do."

"He'll deny that before he's finished," I mumbled.

Sure enough, a few sentences later he said, *"Now here's what you need to do . . ."* He went on to say that we must accept God's grace, and respond to it.

And he's right.

You see, the greatest gift of all—the gift of salvation by grace—doesn't have to be accepted. It can be refused.

Ted Turner's Response

I like Ted Turner.

I know, I know, the brash billionaire—known as *"The Mouth of the South"* and *"Captain Outrageous"*—is notoriously vocal, often obnoxious.

Still, I'm impressed with his never-give-up spirit. Ted, only 24 when his father committed suicide, took over the family's deep-in-debt billboard business. Taking enormous risks, and flouting conventional wisdom, he built a global communications empire! A man of extraordinary energy and talent, Ted is an admirable example of what grit and guts can accomplish.

I like him.

But I cringed at his response to the comment that Jesus had died for his sins. "He needn't have bothered!" snapped Ted.

Appropriating the Gift

A tug-of-war stretches our minds between grace and works. We've been told that grace and works are like oil and water, that one nullifies the other, that a call for obedience is a call for an *earned* salvation.

It's not so.

Obedience is a response to salvation offered, not a striving for salvation earned. Obedience has no earning power, no redeeming power. It has only what C. S. Lewis called "appropriating power."

"Humanity," wrote Lewis, "is already 'saved' in principle. We individuals have to appropriate that salvation."

Jesus won the battle for the *world* when he died. He wins the battle for *your* life when you say "Yes."

The Choice Is Yours

My parents—to whom this book is lovingly dedicated—wanted, more than anything else, for me to believe in Jesus. They provided the teaching and environment that was conducive to producing that belief. But as much as they loved me, they could not believe for me, or confess my faith for me. They could not repent for me, or be baptized for me. The choice was mine alone.

Individual choice is a God-given right—a right that he will not overrule.

God will honor Ted Turner's choice.

And yours. As much as he longs for you to come to him, he won't force it.

Jesus' focus was singular. Every step he took was a step toward the cross. From that cross, with his last breath, he said, *"It is finished!"* He had completed what he came to do.

He didn't come to believe for you, he came to die for you.

He didn't mandate your salvation, but he made it possible.

He won't force it on you, but he offers it.

You choose to accept or reject that offer—to appropriate his gift of grace, or to refuse it.

"Come unto me," he invited. You don't have to. But you can, you know.

AFTERWORD

In the first chapter of this book I told you about Luba Gercak, the compassionate lady who risked her life for 54 children in Germany's Bergen-Belsen concentration camp. Fifty-two of those children survived.

After the war ended Luba moved to the United States and began a new life. She thought often about her children.

They thought about her, too. Stella Degen-Fertig didn't remember much about Bergen-Belsen. But as she grew up, her mother told her how much she owed to a woman named Luba. Stella wondered where she was.

So did others. Jack Rodri told Luba's story on TV. "If anybody knows where she is," he pleaded, "please call this station." Someone did. She lived in Washington, D.C., the caller said.

Gerard Lakmaker, who lived in London, began organizing a tribute to Luba. And on a bright April afternoon in 1995, on the 50th anniversary of their liberation, 30 men and women—most of whom had last seen one another as children at Bergen-Belsen—gathered to honor Luba.

Struggling to control her emotions, Stella Degen-Fertig said to her, "I have thought of you all my life. My mother always told me that she had given birth to me, but that I owed my life to a woman named Luba. She said that I was never to forget it." Weeping, she took Luba into her arms and whispered, "I never will."

I owe my life to my angel mother, but I owe my salvation to Jesus. You and I both do. God help us never to forget it.

I am grateful that you have taken your valuable time to read this book, and I pray that something in these pages has drawn you closer to him. He loves you—and he will never give up on you!

Never?

Never!

NOTES

Chapter 1   What a Night!
1.   Luke 2:9-16
2.   Abridged from Lawrence Elliot. "A Heroine in Hell."
Reader's Digest, November, 1997. pp. 75-78

Chapter 2   The Search Is On
1.   Abridge from Paul Bagne. "Have You Seen This Child."
Reader's Digest, July, 1997. pp. 62-69
2.   The Story of little Rosalie is adapted from Walton's, *A Peep Behind the Scenes.*

Chapter 4   An Arm Around Your Shoulder
1.   Luke 19:1-10

Chapter 5   You Are Special
1.   Adapted from "Teardrops of Hope," By Nancy Sullivan Geng. *Reader's Digest,* September, 1997. pp. 75-77

Chapter 6   A Break Buddy's Advice
1.   This statement is generally credited to Calvin Coolidge.

Chapter 7   Running on the Right Road

1.   Napoleon Hill, *Think & grow Rich* (New York: A Fawcett Crest Book, Published by Ballantine Books, 1996), p. 164.
2.   Ibid., p. 22
3.   C.S. Lewis, Letter of C.S. Lewis. Edited by W.H. Lewis. (New York: Harcourt Brace Jovanovich, 1996), p. 15.

Chapter 8   Fight To The Finish

1.   Gene Shelburn, Anna Street Newsletter, Amarillo, Texas.

Chapter 9   The Hardest Question

1.   Tim Hansel, *You Gotta Keep Dancin* (Elgin, Illinois, Weston, Ontario: David C. Cook Publishing Co. 1995), p. 54.

Chapter 10   To Live in the Light

1.   *The American Heritage Dictionary of the English Language* (New York: American Heritage Publishing Co., Inc., 1969).

Chapter 11   Just Believe

1.   Mark 5:21-43.
2.   George Macdonald, *Malcolm*, as quoted by F.W. Boreham, *A Bunch of Everlastings* (New York, Cincinnati: The Abingdon Press, 1920), p. 11.

Chapter 13   An Unfinished Story

1.   You will find this story in its original form in John 8.

Chapter 14   Bought And Paid For

1.   Harriet Beecher Stowe, *Uncle Tom's Cabin*. Quotations from Easton Press edition, 1979. (My condensation.)
2.   Colossians 1:13-14, Galatians 4:3-5; Matthew 20:28; Ephesians 1:7; Hebrews 9:15.
3.   E.M. Bartlett, *Victory In Jesus*.

Chapter 16   That's Where You Belong
1.   Luke 15:11-31.

Chapter 18   Only One Thing Matters
1.   Adapted from Paul Aurandt, Paul Harvey's The Rest of the Story (A Bantam Book/published by arrangements with Doubleday & Company, Inc., 1977), p. 75.

Chapter 19   It Is Finished
1.   Charles Dickens, *A Tale of Two Cities.*

About the Author

Graduate of Abilene Christian University.

Honorary doctorate from Pepperdine University.

Pulpit minister for Broadway Church of Christ in Lubbock, Texas, for twelve years, at which time it was the second largest church in that fellowship.

Has served on numerous business, civic, and university boards, including Board of Trustees of Lubbock Christian University, and Board of Regent of Pepperdine University.

Was editor of *20th Century Christian* Magazine for 10 years.
Was a featured speaker on nationally syndicated *Herald of Truth* television programs for five years.

Hosted the nationally broadcast prime-time television special, *The Pursuit of Happiness.*

Has spoken in every state and several countries.
Has written or co-written ten books, dozens of pamphets, and hundreds or articles.

Founder and president of Pathway Evangelism, Inc., a non-profit organization which distributes Christian literature.

Founder and president of Pathway Publishing House, Inc., which publishes literature for church distriution.